6524

DATE DUE

Metro Litho
Oak Forest, IL 60452

SEP 1 8 1992			
SEP 2 5 1992			
OCT 0 5 1992			
MAR 1 8 1993			

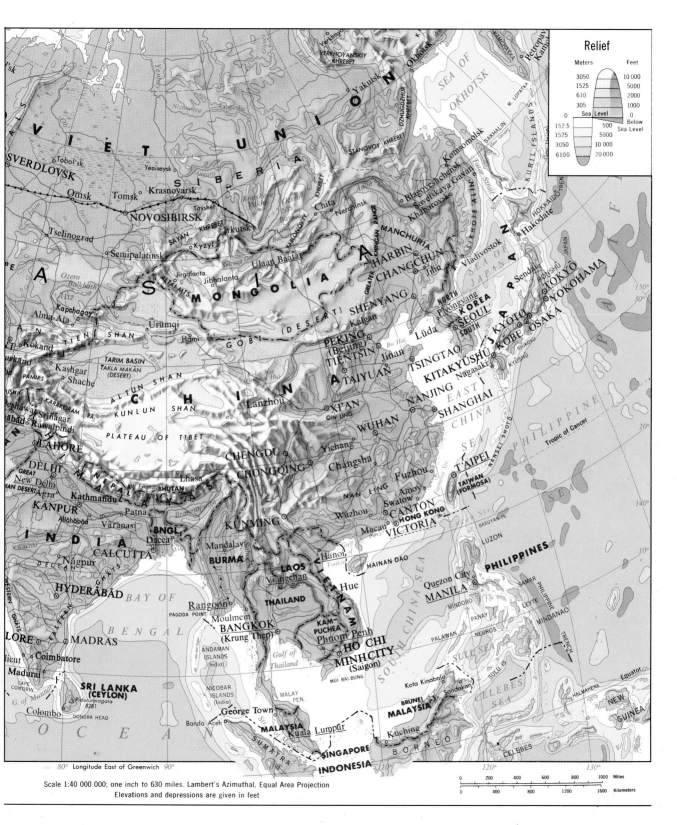

Relief

Meters		Feet
3050		10 000
1525		5000
610		2000
305		1000
Sea Level		0
		Below
152.5		500 Sea Level
1525		5000
3050		10 000
6100		20 000

Scale 1:40 000 000; one inch to 630 miles. Lambert's Azimuthal, Equal Area Projection
Elevations and depressions are given in feet

80° Longitude East of Greenwich 90°

| 0 | 200 | 400 | 600 | 800 | 1000 | Miles |

| 0 | 400 | 800 | 1200 | 1600 | Kilometers |

Birobidžan Smidovič · Korfovskij · Nevel'skii · Adimi
DA HINGGAN LING · JAN LING · Leninskoje · Vjazemskii · Gornozavodsk · La Perouse Strait · OSTROV KUNAŠIR
Hailar Nunjiang · Iman · Korsakov · zaliv · Aniva · Wakkanai · SHIRETOKO MISAKI · Mombetsu · Abashiri
Hailar · Nane · Yichun · Fulin · Svetlaja · REBUN-TO · Nayoro · Yūbari · Kitami · Nemuro
Nur · Bei'an · RISHIRI-TO · Rumoi · Asahikawa · △ Asahidake · Kushiro
Butha Qi · Balin · HEILONGJIANG · Hegang · Bikin · Ternej · Otaru · 2290 · Obihiro · HOKKAIDŌ
Longjiang · Ergun · HEILUNGKIANG · Hailun · Jiamusi · Shuangyashan · Dal'nerečensk · Lesozovodsk · Sapporo · Tomakomai · 145°
Qiqihar · Tsitsihar · Anda · Hulan · Mishan · Xingkai Hu · Spassk-Dal'nij · Muroran · Uchiura-Wan
Baicheng · MANCHURIA · Harbin · Acheng · Shangzhi · Pogranicnyi · Ussurijsk · Hakodate · Mutsu
Horqin Youyi Qianqi · Fuyu · Shuangcheng · Linkou · Art'om · Aomori · Hachinohe
Arxan · Solon · Dehui · Jiutai · Dunhua · Tumen · Yanji · Vladivostok · Nachodka · Hirosaki · Miyako
Changchun · Huaide · Jiaohe · Hunchun · Posjet · Najin · Noshiro · Akita · Kamaishi
Tongliao · Siping · Liaoyuan · Huadian · Ch'ŏngjin · Akita · Ishinomaki
GOL · ZIZHIQU · JILIN · KIRIN · Paektu-san · Nairam · SADO · Sakata · Tsuruoka · Yamagata · Sendai
Xar Moron · Kaiyuan · Tonghua · 2744 · Hyesan · Kimch'aek · Nanao · Joetsu · Yonezawa
Fuxin · SHENYANG · Fushun · Kanggye · NORTH · Niigata · Aizu-wakamatsu · Iwaki
Beipiao · MUKDEN · Tonghua · KOREA · Hamhung · Hüngnam · Toyama · Nagano · Maebashi · Mito
Chaoyang · Liaoyang · Anshan · Benxi · Hüich'ŏn · Wŏnsan · Kanazawa · Matsumoto · Utsunomiya
Jinzhou · Haicheng · Anju · Sŏkch'o · Fukui · Gifu · Kōfu · TŌKYŌ
Yingkou · LIAONING · Sinüiju · P'yŏngyang · Ch'unch'ŏn · Kanazawa · Nagoya · Kawasaki · Yokohama
Dandong · Namp'o · Songnim · Kaesŏng · Sŏul SEOUL · Toyohashi · Shizuoka · Yokosuka
Jinxian · Lüshun · Lüda · Inch'ŏn · SOUTH · Matsue · Himeji · Kyōto · Kōbe · Nara · Hamamatsu
Port Arthur · Dairen · Haeju · Suwŏn · KOREA · Okayama · ŌSAKA · Wakayama
Qinhuangdao · Tangshan · Bo Hai · Ch'ŏnan · Andong · Kurashiki · Kure · Takamatsu · Tokushima
TIANJIN · Cangzhou · Taejŏn · Kyŏngju · Hiroshima · Matsuyama · Kōchi
TIENTSIN · Weihai · Chŏnju · P'ohang · Ube · Shimonoseki · SHIKOKU
Boshan · Yantai · Chŏngju · Masan · Kitakyūshū · Fukuoka · Kurume · Ōita
Qingdao · Tsingtao · Kwangju · Sunch'ŏn · Pusan · Sasebo · Kumamoto · Miyazaki
Weifang · Mokp'o · Yŏsu · Nagasaki · Ōmuta · KYŪSHŪ · Miyakonojō
Lianyungang · Cheju · Halla-san · Kagoshima · Nichinan
JIANGSU · KIANGSU · 1950 · CHEJU-DO · SATA-MISAKI
Huaiyin · Yancheng · Nanjing · Zhenjiang · Nantong · SHANGHAI · EAST · CHINA · SEA
Hefei · Changzhou · Suzhou · Wuxi
Wuhu · ANHUI · Hangzhou · ZHEJIANG · Ningbo
Wenzhou · Fuzhou

Enchantment of the World

JAPAN

By Carol Greene

Consultants: Mrs. Oda, Japanese Consulate, Chicago, Illinois

Stephen Burke, Undergraduate Asian Studies, University of Michigan, Ann Arbor

Consultant for Social Studies: Donald W. Nylin, Ph.D., Assistant Superintendent for Instruction, Aurora West Public Schools, Aurora, Illinois

Consultant for Reading: Robert L. Hillerich, Ph.D., Bowling Green State University, Bowling Green, Ohio

 CHILDRENS PRESS, CHICAGO

Two young girls wear summer kimonos called yukatas.

This book is for Beth and with special thanks to Patricia Babcock of Yokohama

Library of Congress Cataloging in Publication Data

Greene, Carol.
  Japan.

  (The Enchantment of the world)
  Includes index.
  Summary: Describes some of Japan's features in the areas of geography, history, scenic treasures, culture, industry, and people.
  1. Japan—Juvenile literature. [1. Japan] I. Title. II. Series.
DS806.G73 1983   952   83-7603
ISBN 0-516-02769-7   AACR2

Picture Acknowledgments

Hillstrom Stock Photos: © Norma Morrison: 4, 10, 15 (left), 16, 20, 23 (bottom), 26, 28 (right), 32, 33 (2 photos), 35 (bottom), 36, 37, 44 (right), 46 (bottom left), 52, 84 (left), 86, 96, 102 (2 photos), 103, 104, 106, 107, 109; © M.R. David: 35 (top), 57; © Milton and Joan Mann: 45 (right), 48 (top and bottom)
© **Chandler Forman:** 9, 38
© **Jerome Wyckoff:** 40 (top)
© **Joseph Antos:** 40 (bottom)
Gladys J. Peterson: 15 (right), 39, 67, 71 (right), 93 (left)
Root Resources: © E. Simms, 12, 34 (bottom); © Jane Shepstone, 24, 42, 43
Color Library International: Cover, 5, 6, 14, 19 (2 photos), 21, 23 (top), 27, 28 (left), 29, 30, 34 (top), 45 (left) 48, 72 (left), 85, 93 (right), 95 (left), 101, 121
Historical Pictures Services, Chicago: 50, 59, 69, 74
Japan National Tourist Organization: 11 (right), 44 (left), 46 (top, bottom right), 49, 60, 62, 63, 71 (left), 80, 84 (right), 87, 95 (right), 99, 108
The Metropolitan Museum of Art: Bequest of Stephen Whitney Phoenix, 1881, 11 (left); Bequest of George C. Stone, 1936, 76; The Henry L. Phillips Collection. Bequest of Henry L. Phillips, 1940, 88; Gift of Elizabeth Gordon, 1967, 90
Courtesy Flag Research Center, Winchester, Massachusetts 01890: Flag on back cover
Cover: Nagasaki Harbor

Vistors leave Kannon Temple in Toyko.

TABLE OF CONTENTS

Himeji Castle

Chapter 1

THE LAND OF
THE RISING SUN

A FAIRY-TALE COUNTRY

Japan. A country far away, isn't it? In the Far East? And very different? Sometimes called the Land of the Rising Sun? It sounds like a fairy-tale country. How does such a place look? What are its people like?

In some ways Japan *is* a fairy-tale country. One moment you struggle through a forest of concrete and neon in Tokyo. The next moment you're lost in a cloud of cherry blossoms as the moon laughs down at you. You zoom through city streets filled with a buzzing swarm of traffic. You walk through a park while a silent swarm of butterflies floats overhead.

A fairy-tale country. A country of legends and festivals, waiting dogs and living treasures, paper cranes and nervous goblins. Japan's a wonderful country to visit. And its people are ready and eager to make visitors feel welcome.

THE WAITING DOG AND THE BECKONING CAT

In a plaza by a subway station in Tokyo sits the statue of a dog. Once a real dog sat there. His name was Hachiko. His master had died, but the dog waited for him every day for years. Passersby fed him. Finally the dog died, too. The dog became known as Chuken (Loyal Dog) Hachiko and will be remembered long by the Japanese people. Loyalty and faithfulness are important in Japan.

In some Tokyo restaurants and shops are figures of a cat with one paw raised. It's known as "the beckoning cat." The real beckoning cat belonged to a priest in the 1600s. The priest's temple was very poor. One day the cat went out to sit by its main gate. When a rich man rode by, the cat raised its paw and beckoned to him. The man stopped, went inside, and from then on gave money to the temple. Japanese merchants hope their beckoning cat figures will help their businesses succeed, too. Success is also important in Japan.

A LONG MEMORY

A group of Japanese goblins once decided to make ninety-nine valleys. Night after night they worked. (Goblins don't like daylight.) They had just finished the ninety-eighth valley late one night when the rising sun caught them by surprise. Off they ran. But one of the little goblins was so nervous that he left behind the cartload of earth he'd been pushing. You can still see it. It's a low hill near Lake Haruna and it's called Hitomokko ("The Cartload of Earth")

Traditional costumes are an important part of most festivals.

Japanese people love to remember and tell old legends like this. They also love to hold festivals. Sometimes the legends and the festivals get mixed up together.

There's a tale of two stars in the sky that fell in love. They wanted to get married. But the girl star's father said no. He didn't even want them to meet. So he spread out the Milky Way between them. After a while, though, his heart softened. He decided the two lovers could meet across the Milky Way just once a year—on July 7.

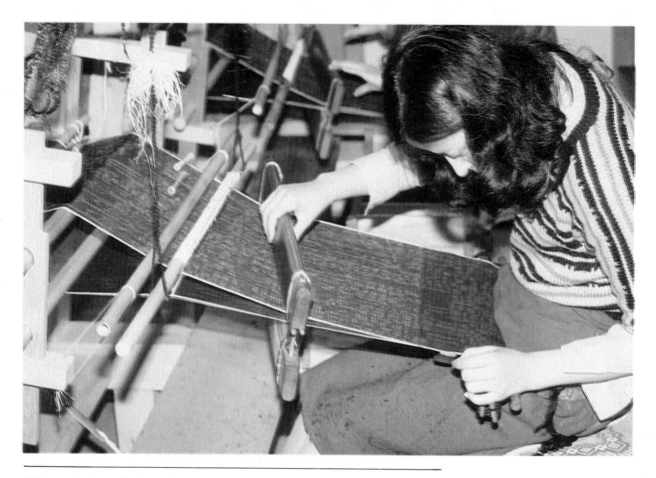

This particular technique of weaving silk is limited to the town of Yuki, Japan.

The Japanese celebrate this meeting of the starry lovers each July 7 with a festival called *Tanabata*. They decorate bamboo poles with strips of colored paper and folded paper figures and display them outside their homes. And the two stars look down and know that the earth shares their happiness.

Japanese people try to remember the ways of the past, too. They're especially careful to protect the old ways of making beautiful things. The Japanese government has named more than seventy older artists and craftspeople "living national treasures." (Their official title is "Holders of Important Intangible Cultural Properties.")

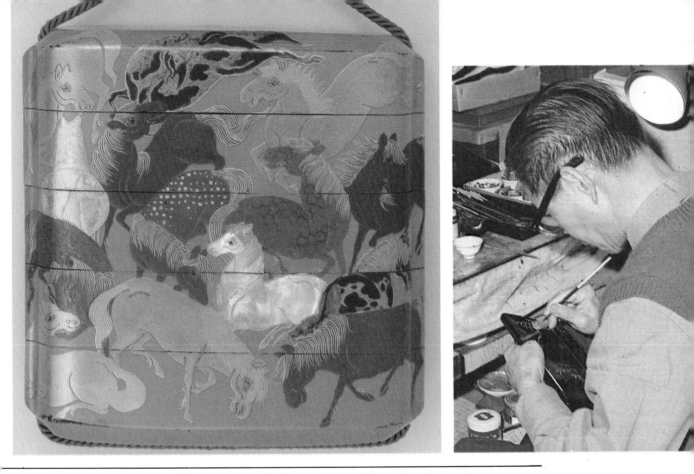

An artist (right) works on his lacquer ware. This early nineteenth century lacquer piece (left) is called The Hundred Horses. The red background has gold and silver lacquer (takamakiye) with decorations in high relief and shell.

Some of these people weave cloth. Some make pottery. Some make and use puppets. Some are swordsmiths, dyers, and lacquer workers. The government gives financial aid to these living treasures. In return, they teach what they know to younger people.

And what exactly do they teach? The skill of their art, of course. But lacquer artist Gonroku Matsuda says that skill is not enough. ''Spirit is the essential quality behind great art,'' he says, ''a spirit that demands an endless search for perfection. And that spirit must be developed, layer on layer, like fine lacquer work.''

Outdoor art class meets in Nara, Japan.

A HYMN TO LIFE

''The earth is the Mother of all creatures.
She gives them life and they give her songs.
Great trees and tiny herbs, stones, sand, and soil,
Winds and waves—all have a soul.
Woodland breezes in spring, buzzing insects in fall
—all sing their songs to the Earth.
The breeze's sigh and the torrent's roar
—both are hymns to life.
Let all livings things rejoice in this!''

This is a hymn from Shinto, Japan's oldest religion. Nature plays a big part in Shinto and in the lives of all Japanese people, no matter what their religion. In nature they find peace and harmony, beauty and meaning. Their gardens and flowering trees are dear to them. So are their rugged mountains and towering waves.

As you look at one perfect Japanese plum blossom or watch the sun stain Mount Fuji pink and gold, stop for a moment. Listen carefully. It might be that you, too, will hear it—the hymn to life sung by all of nature's creations.

DIFFERENT?

In some ways Japan is different from many other places in the world. For example, it is a land where a young girl can grow up to be a *geisha* (GAY-shah). Geisha are professional entertainers. They usually perform at private gatherings in specially designed buildings.

In order to be a geisha, a girl must learn the traditional way of dancing, singing, playing musical instruments, making

Girl models the elaborate makeup and colorful kimono worn by a geisha.

conversation, and serving food and drink. She doesn't have to be especially pretty, because she'll be heavily made up, but she will have to be very charming.

But Japan is also a land where a young girl can wander down the street in designer jeans and T-shirt, listening to rock music on her transistor radio. She can dream of becoming a doctor or a poet, a college professor or a newspaper reporter. And she can make her dream come true.

In a small Japanese village, an older Japanese woman might be patiently folding bright paper into the shape of a crane. She's practicing the ancient Japanese art of paper folding, known as

Toyko policewoman (left) symbolizes modern Japan. The woman hanging up paper cranes (symbols of long life and happiness) keeps alive a tradition hundreds of years old.

origami. She'll make a thousand of the birds. Many paper cranes are strung together and called Senbazuru. Senbazuru is considered a symbol of long life and happiness. When people pray to God for something, they often make this string of paper cranes.

But the woman doesn't put all her faith in paper cranes. When she is ill, she calls a doctor.

That woman is like people in other countries who carry a four-leaf clover for good luck and yet also buy insurance policies. She's a good symbol for Japan. In many ways Japan is different from the rest of the world. But in many ways it's the same.

North coast of the Sea of Japan

Chapter 2

A LAND FROM THE SEA

THE STORY TOLD BY LEGEND

Many years ago, the earth was nothing but a great ball of water. Over it arched a rainbow and on the rainbow stood the god Izanagi. Izanagi reached down and dipped his spear into the water. Then he raised it. Drops of water fell back to the earth and turned into islands of many sizes.

I have created a beautiful land, thought Izanagi. So he and his sister, Izanami, left heaven. And, for a time, they lived in the beautiful land—Japan.

THE STORY TOLD BY SCIENCE

In a way, the Japanese islands really were born from the sea. But they didn't drop from the spear of a god. Instead, tremendous movements of the earth millions of years ago shoved giant, volcanic mountains up out of the sea. The tops of these mountains are now the islands of Japan.

Japan is made up of four main islands and many smaller ones. The largest is Honshu. About 79 percent of Japan's people live on Honshu. To the north is Hokkaido, the second largest island, with 5 percent of the people. Kyushu, the third largest island and the one farthest south, has 12 percent of the people. And tucked between Kyushu and Honshu is Shikoku, the smallest main island. Only 3.5 percent of the Japanese people live on Shikoku.

Japan also owns the Ryukyu and Bonin islands. The Ryukyus are a chain of about one hundred islands. They run from Kyushu to Taiwan. The largest of the Ryukyu Islands is Okinawa. The Bonin Islands are between Honshu and Guam. There are ninety-seven small islands in this chain.

People often think of Japan as a small country. But that's true only in comparison with huge countries such as Russia, Australia, and the United States. Japan's 145,834 square miles (377,708 square kilometers) make her about the size of East and West Germany combined. If the Japanese islands were placed next to the eastern coast of the United States, they'd run from Maine down to Georgia.

TOPS OF THE MOUNTAINS

The very tops of the mountains that make up Japan form her mountains and hills. These spread across about 72 percent of all the land in Japan. Many of them are covered with forests, dotted with lakes, and crisscrossed with busy little rivers and streams. They're beautiful—and fun to explore.

But all those mountains don't make farming an easy job. Most of them are in the middle of the islands. So the people live

Lake Nojiri and Mount Myoko (above) and this Shirakawa village (below) are in the Japanese Alps on the island of Honshu.

Earth dam at a hydroelectric plant in the Japanese Alps

crowded together around the coastal edges. Farmers grow crops on whatever bits of flat land they can find. All in all, they have only about 15 percent of the total land area to use.

Japan's mountains don't hold many mineral resources, either. There is some coal, but not much else. But the Japanese have found a different sort of treasure in their mountains—water power. They have harnessed those busy rivers and streams to make electricity and to water the lowlands.

About two hundred of Japan's mountains are volcanoes. Some are still active. The most famous is Mount Fuji, an inactive volcano on Honshu. Mount Fuji (called Fujisan) soars 12,388 feet

Mount Fuji is an inactive volcano.

(3,776 meters) above sea level. It is the highest point in Japan. The volcano last erupted in 1707. Now it stands quiet, a symbol of the beauty of Japan. Sightseers can climb right up to the crater's rim.

These mountains in the sea that make up Japan are not very old as mountains go. This gives the Japanese people another problem—earthquakes. As the mountains shift and settle, the eastern coasts of Japan are pushed up higher out of the sea. The western coasts sink into the water.

Japan has about fifteen hundred earthquakes each year. Most are small, but some aren't. In 1923, an earthquake killed 99,331 people in Tokyo and Yokohama. In 1964, a quake did much damage to Niigata, but it killed only a few people.

A PLACE FOR PEOPLE

Japan has a diverse climate.

Hokkaido, the northern island, has seasons much like those in New England. Winters are cold and snowy and summers are cool.

Honshu, the middle island, has a climate more like North Carolina's. Spring and fall are long and sunny. Summer is warm and wet. Winter is mild—in the south. But in northern Honshu blustery winds blow in from Siberia. They bring cold and a lot of snow.

Kyushu and Shikoku lie farthest south. Their climate is more like that of Georgia or Florida. Summers are long and hot and winters are mild.

Japan is in the monsoon belt. That means that twice a year (early summer and early fall) heavy rains called monsoons come in on winds from the sea. The rain is welcomed by Japan's farmers, especially the rice growers. But another gift from the sea winds isn't so popular. It's the typhoon, a fierce cyclone storm that can cause much damage.

Japan's climate is partly the result of two ocean currents. The Japan Current flows northward along the southern and eastern coasts and brings warmer conditions to southern Japan. The other current, the cold Oyashio, flows southward. It influences the climate of western Hokkaido and northern Honshu.

For the most part, Japan's climate is a good one for her people. Growing seasons are long enough and wet enough for crops. People don't have to waste time battling the weather. In fact, some scholars say Japan's climate is the most important geographical feature helping to make her a strong, prosperous nation.

Winters are cold and snowy in the northern part of the island of Honshu, but its summers are warm. Rice, the country's most important crop, is grown on each of Japan's four main islands.

Inland Sea as seen from an island

WATER, WATER, EVERYWHERE!

From a tiny garden pool to her own private sea, Japan treasures her water. There are no long rivers. The longest, the Shinano, is only 229 miles (368 kilometers) long. But the short rivers and streams do a good job of watering crops and generating electricity.

Japan also has many lakes and hot springs. The largest lake, Lake Biwa, is on Honshu. It covers 265 square miles (673.8 square kilometers). Thousands of smaller lakes lie like blue and silver patches in the mountains. The Japanese people love to vacation at resorts alongside their lakes.

Most important, of course, are the oceans that surround Japan and make her an island nation. To the west lies the Sea of Japan. It separates Japan from Russia, China, and Korea. To the east and south is the Pacific Ocean.

Korea is Japan's closest neighbor. The water between the two countries is about 100 miles (161 kilometers) wide at its narrowest spot. About 600 miles (965 kilometers) of water lie between Japan and China. These distances are short in today's world. But for hundreds of years, the sea was like a giant moat that isolated Japan from almost everything and everyone else in the world. This gave Japan a chance to become independent and grow strong before other countries began to influence her.

Japan is also the proud possessor of her own sea. It's called the Inland Sea and lies between Honshu and the two southern islands. About three thousand little tree-covered islands dot this sea and make it a beautiful place to visit. But the Inland Sea is also an important waterway for the Japanese.

Japan has long coastlines because her shores are so jagged. The coastlines around the four main islands total about 5,857 miles (9,426 kilometers). Because the mountains provide few resources,

25

Like other industrialized nations, Japan has a shortage of housing. However, despite crowded conditions, this tiny garden flourishes in an urban setting.

Japan has always turned to the coasts for a living. Fishing has been—and still is—an important source of food and income. In recent times, Japan's coastal ports have also become doorways for trade with the rest of the world.

SMALLER TREASURES

The Japanese people love nature. They write poems about dragonflies, crickets, or sparrows. They plan and tend gardens until they are as perfect as polished jewels. They carefully arrange cut flowers according to ancient rules. Perhaps part of their love and care comes from the fact that they have so little land on which to enjoy nature's smaller treasures.

Cedar, maple, oak, and pine trees grow in Japan and are used for lumber. Many poplar trees grow on Hokkaido. Mulberry trees are used in the production of silk. Apple trees are grown in the north, and pear, orange, and tangerine trees in the south. Their fruits are an important crop.

Picnics are held when the cherry blossoms bloom.

But Japan's most famous trees are grown simply for their beauty and produce no fruit. These are the cherry trees that burst into clouds of pink blossoms each spring in gardens and along paths and avenues. Beneath them the Japanese people have a gay flower-viewing party called *Hanami*.

Other favorite garden trees are pine trees and plums. The plums serve two purposes: they offer blossoms and they give fruit. Japanese people pickle their plums, and sometimes they make plum wine.

But not all of Japan's blossoms are on trees. Flowers grow wherever a flower can be coaxed to grow. They include irises, tulips, forsythia, violets, morning glories, peonies, camellias, roses, hibiscus, daffodils, poppies, hollyhocks, rose of Sharon, bush-clover, lotus, and lilies (both Easter and water). In the south, orchids grow well and so do cacti and hibiscus.

Perhaps Japan's favorite flower, though, is the chrysanthemum. Japanese poets have written about chrysanthemums for centuries.

Tame deer roam freely in a nature center in Nara. On the right is a chrysanthemum display.

Japanese painters have painted them for just as long. The crest of
the imperial family itself is a golden chrysanthemum with sixteen
petals.

Many kinds of birds make their home in Japan, including geese
and ducks, hawks, eagles, quail, pheasant, plover, gulls,
cormorants, swans, storks, herons, cranes, crows, starlings, owls,
whippoorwills, swallows, nightingales, cuckoos, woodpeckers,
larks, bobolinks, wrens, and sparrows.

Then there are the insects: butterflies and moths, dragonflies,
other flies, bees, crickets, grasshoppers, cicadas, mosquitoes, gnats,
and many others. Of course, not even the nature-loving Japanese
like all these insects. But they are fond of some kinds. Fireflies,
which used to be common, are now rare, especially around cities.
And the Japanese miss them.

The forests of Japan still hold deer. Sometimes, in the heart of a
forest, a few bears can be seen. Wild monkeys live in a few places.

Rural farm in Shikazawa Heights

Toads hop around in the country and frogs sing their grumpy songs from the lakes.

Throughout the country are the usual farm animals—cows, pigs, and chickens. And people everywhere care for household pets—cats, dogs, parrots, goldfish, hamsters, and even chipmunks.

THAT'S JAPAN

An island country, perched on mountains and surrounded by a silver moat of sea. That's Japan. A land of gentle climate, where both crops and people can thrive. That's Japan, too. A land of thick green forests, bright blue lakes, and blossoms of every color. That's Japan.

Is it really a land created by the god Izanagi while standing on a rainbow? Or does it just look that way?

The Ginza in downtown Tokyo

Chapter 3

A LAND OF WONDERS

TOKYO!

Tokyo is a city of skyscrapers and Shinto shrines. It is a city of flashing neon lights and glowing paper lanterns. It is city of *sushi* (raw fish on rice balls) and Kentucky Fried Chicken. Most of all, it is a city of growth.

Two thousand years ago, a nobleman called Dokan Ota built a fort at the spot where several rivers meet and empty into Tokyo Bay. He called his fort Edo, which means "estuary." A village grew up around that fort.

Then, around 1600, the military leader Tokugawa Ieyasu decided that Edo should be the capital of Japan. In 1868, the city's name was changed to Tokyo (eastern capital).

The site of Dokan Ota's fort is where the Imperial Palace stands today. Most people consider it the center of the city. Around the palace sparkles a necklace of ponds and streams that used to be a moat. Ducks and swans swim on their waters.

Willow trees at the Imperial Palace, Toyko

Beyond the ponds and streams stretches a huge, oval-shaped park, dotted with small, twisted pines and tall, graceful willows. On chilly winter days, sea gulls pour into this park to roost. That might be why Japanese people call gulls "capital birds."

But all year round, visitors pour into Tokyo. It's a very popular place for both foreign and Japanese tourists. Sometimes these visitors have a hard time finding their way around the city. That's because of the way Tokyo grew. At first it was simply a village surrounded by many other villages. But as its population grew, these villages all blended together. Country roads became city streets. Farm cottages found themselves next to concrete office buildings. Streets often were not named. Even today, street names don't mean much in Tokyo. House numbers tell when a house was built, not where it is. And today Tokyo is the second largest city in the world.

Small shops (above) sell many items, but large,
modern supermarkets (below) also attract customers.

Above: High-speed
monorail trains bring
workers into the city every day.
The Tokyo Tower is one
of the city's landmarks.
At the central market (left)
bikes, trucks, and cars are
used to transport goods.
Toyko's shops in the
Asakusa section (opposite top)
are loaded with goods and
customers. Street crews
(opposite bottom) are used to
keep the city clean.

Yasakuni Shrine honors all those who fought and died for Japan.

But the Japanese people do all they can to help visitors in Tokyo. They take being good hosts very seriously. Many of them speak English. And they have kept street crime to a minimum.

Tokyo has its share of factories, businesses, and communications centers. Trade centers display many of Japan's exports, including machines, machine tools, plastics, and other goods. But skyscrapers are fairly new. Until recently, buildings weren't supposed to be over seven stories tall. That was because Tokyo has so many earthquakes, although most are minor. Now new building methods permit taller buildings.

Since Tokyo is a harbor city, many fishing boats put in there. At the fish market in the Tsukiji (Skee-jee) section of the city, almost every kind of fish—including shark—is sold.

There is a lot to see and do in Tokyo at night.

Having fun is also a business in Tokyo. Tourism is one of Japan's most important industries and tourists want to have fun. In Tokyo, they can shop in the Asakusa section. Shops along the maze of little alleys and covered passages sell everything from stuffed peacocks to cameras. Tired shoppers can enjoy a meal in a restaurant, tea in a teahouse, a soak in a bathhouse, or a ride on a merry-go-round.

At night, the Ginza and Shimbashi sections of the city are like a vast, neon playground, full of nightclubs, cabarets, bars, restaurants, and eating stalls.

Both the Japanese and tourists like to visit Summerland all year round. It's a building with a huge glass dome. Inside the temperature is always balmy. Guests swim in artificial surf or lie on artificial beaches. Summerland is just one more surprise in the surprising city of Tokyo.

Statue of Buddha at Kamakura

A CRESCENT OF PLEASURE

The Chiba-Kanto area is like a crescent of pleasure cupped around Tokyo. Mountains, countryside, interesting villages, and the sea all provide playgrounds for both Japanese people and tourists. And nothing is more than a few hours from the city by bus or train.

Narita, like many places in Japan, is a mixture of old and new. A gleaming international airport welcomes many visitors to the town. But in January, they will find crowds of religious pilgrims making their way to the Shinshoji Temple, which was built to honor a priest who brought a sacred image there.

These pilgrims eat holiday foods, such as roast chestnuts and cotton candy. But they also pray and pour icy water over themselves each morning in penance for the wrongs they've done.

Grand prize winner in a bonsai contest

Nikko

Omiya

Chichibu   Tokyo   Mito

Narita

Yokohama

Mt.
Fuji   Kamakura

Folk crafts have always been important to Japan, both for use at home and for export. In the Chiba-Kanto area nestle many little villages where these crafts are still practiced.

At Mashiko lives a colony of potters. Shoji Hamada, one of the "living national treasures," worked here. Near Omiya, tiny bonsai trees—some only inches high—decorate village homes and sell for tremendous prices. At Ogawa-machi, paper has been made from mulberry bark for over a thousand years. And at Chichibu, workers weave silk.

Two other big cities lie close enough to Tokyo that workers can commute each day. One is Kamakura, famous for its giant statue of Buddha and its thousand-year-old ginkgo tree. Kamakura was Japan's capital for 150 years and visitors can still absorb history in its shrines, temples, and museums. Or they can play on its noisy beaches. (It's been called "the Coney Island of Japan.")

In Nikko, a national park, visitors can go to a
Shinto Shrine (above) or the Buddhist Temple (below).

Commuters to Tokyo also live in the quiet city of Yokohama. This city has had a rough history. An earthquake leveled it in 1923. A firebomb raid leveled it again in 1945. But each time Yokohama has been rebuilt and today it's the second largest city in Japan.

About an hour's drive from Tokyo lies Fuji-Hakone-Izu National Park, home of great Mount Fuji and Lake Hakone. Each weekend, people rush from the city to camp, swim, boat, skate, ride, hike, hunt, fish, water-ski, take the waters of the hot springs, or just relax. Unfortunately, much of the land has been developed into big, commercial amusement areas. It isn't as beautiful as it used to be.

But Mount Fuji, an extinct volcano, still looms above its five lakes, a lovely and powerful symbol to the Japanese people. At one time Mount Fuji was considered to be sacred. Its image still appears in much of Japan's arts and crafts.

Some hardy people climb the mountain. It takes seven to nine hours to get to the top and two to five hours to get back down. But sunrise from Mount Fuji is said to be an incredible sight.

Another national park, close enough for a day's sightseeing from Tokyo, is Nikko. Here lie the remains of one of Japan's most powerful military leaders, Tokugawa Ieyasu. Ieyasu was a clever man. He knew that if he kept his men busy and broke, they wouldn't be as likely to give him trouble. So he set them to building his tomb. The result is one of the most unusual works of art anywhere.

Giant cedars tower over temples and shrines, mausoleums, gates, a pagoda, storehouses, a drum tower, a library, a dance stage, covered corridors, and more. Many of the buildings are covered with gold leaf, enough to stretch over six acres. Some visitors say that just looking at the Sun Gate, carved with every sort of creature, was enough to wear them out.

Looking over the rooftops on Sado Island towards the Sea of Japan

TO THE NORTH

Mountains are a problem for Japan. Since they take up over four fifths of the country, the people are mostly squeezed into the remaining area. But Japan's mountains are also beautiful, especially her Alps in the northern half of the island of Honshu. And the Japanese people are learning to enjoy them more and more. In winter, sports lovers ski. In summer they climb or just cool off. In any season they revel in the treasures of nature.

Sado is an island in the Sea of Japan. Prisoners used to be sent there to work in the gold mines. But today travelers on their way north stop instead to see the waterfalls, the flying fish, and the rare Japanese crested ibis, a bird that is almost extinct.

This Ainu woman in traditional dress lives on Hokkaido Island.

Also in the north is Matsushima. Matsushima is an archipelago, a group of hundreds of islands. Some are tiny and some are large enough to live on. All are covered with twisted pines and all have been strangely etched and carved by the sea.

Still farther north is Japan's second largest island—Hokkaido. It's a rugged place with deep lakes, bears, and Japan's newest volcano, Showa Shinzan. (It was born in 1944.) Hokkaido is a good place for cattle and produces most of Japan's dairy products.

Hokkaido is also the home of most of the Ainu people. They were some of Japan's earliest settlers. Their culture did not develop as fully as that of the later settlers. Slowly—and sometimes painfully—the Ainu are being absorbed by the people around them. But some of their villages still remain on Hokkaido.

Nagoya Castle (left) and a crowded street in Kyoto (right)

IN THE MIDDLE

The center of Honshu is the home of some important and fascinating Japanese cities. About 160 miles (257 kilometers) southwest of Tokyo lies Nagoya, a city heavily damaged during World War II. But Nagoya, like other Japanese cities, has been rebuilt and today is a center of industry. In fact, as the city expands, its developers have begun reclaiming land from the sea at Ise Bay. World-famous Noritake china is just one of the many goods manufactured in Nagoya.

About 160 miles (257 kilometers) west of Nagoya is the grand old city of Kyoto, sometimes called "the spiritual heart of Japan." It was laid out in 794 like a Chinese city. Some of that old city plan still remains, even though the city itself was burned down during the 1400s.

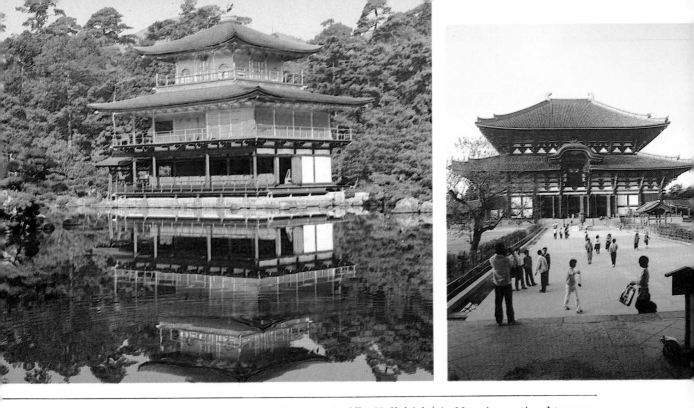

Golden Pavilion (above) is in Kyoto. The Great Buddha Hall (right) in Nara is a national treasure.

Modern Kyoto includes industrial, trade, and educational centers. But in older parts of the city, great monuments to the past still stand. One of these is Nijo Castle, built in 1603. It looks very much like a Western castle from the outside, with all its turrets and moats. Inside, though, big gardens stretch between wooden buildings that are filled with Japanese art.

Visitors to one of the main buildings are often surprised to discover that the floors were made to squeak, no matter how softly someone may walk. They were made that way to warn people inside the building of intruders. The same clever Tokugawa Ieyasu who kept his men busy building his tomb also came up with this idea.

A short distance from Kyoto lies Nara, Japan's first capital, a city filled with religious shrines. One of these is Todai-ji (East Great Temple), the largest wooden structure in the world. Here, in

45

Downtown Osaka (above) and Bunraku puppets
(below). The Peace Monument at Hiroshima
in the distance is the shell of a building left
standing after the atomic bomb was
dropped on the city.

the Great Buddha Hall, sits the Great Sun Buddha, a figure 71.5 inches (183.8 centimeters) tall. Buddhists believe that the Great Sun Buddha's body contains everything in the universe and that everything comes from him.

Close to Nara is Osaka, a city that has bustled with trade for hundreds of years. Actually, Kyoto, Nara, and Osaka almost form one giant city. Together they are responsible for one fourth of Japan's industrial output, one third of her trade, and two fifths of her exports. Main industries include printing, food processing, textiles, and chemical and heavy industries.

About 170 miles (274 kilometers) west of Osaka is the city of Hiroshima. Here, on August 6, 1945, the United States exploded the first atomic bomb ever used in war. Not everyone in the city died. But those who still survive don't like to talk about what happened. "Peace" is an important word in Hiroshima. Visitors today find Peace Park, Peace Memorial Hall, and the Peace Memorial Museum, which contains relics of the bombing. Hiroshima is a rebuilt city. It's also a city to make you think.

TO THE SOUTH

The Inland Sea lies in the southern part of Japan, surrounded by Honshu, Kyushu, and Shikoku. The sea itself is famous for its Naruto Whirlpools, which swirl four times a day because of changes in the tide. Sometimes the pools are 75 feet (22.8 meters) in diameter and their roar is tremendous.

Shikoku is Japan's smallest main island. It includes lovely parks and the Ritsurin Zoo. Archaeologists have found the ruins of Japan's largest ancient settlement on Shikoku. Bird lovers rush to the city of Kochi where roosters have tails over 20 feet (6 meters) long.

Rice is harvested by machine on the island of Kyushu.

Mount Aso is an active volcano.

Farthest south of the main islands is Kyushu, a warm place filled with warm people. Kyushu was the first island to greet people from the West. Dutch people had a trading post there for hundreds of years. The Christian missionary St. Francis Xavier also landed on Kyushu.

Nagasaki, one of the chief cities on Kyushu, was where the world's second atomic bomb was dropped. It destroyed Japan's largest Christian church, which was later rebuilt by Nagasaki Catholics.

Kyushu is also the home of Mount Aso, the world's largest active volcano. Visitors can go right up to the edge and look in. The kind people of Kyushu have provided little concrete huts by the volcano to hide in should Aso erupt.

North, middle, or south—Japan is rich in history, industry, and natural treasures.

In Japanese mythology Nikke is the thunder god.

Chapter 4

A LAND ALONE

THE STORY TOLD BY LEGEND

After living in Japan for a while, Izanagi and Izanami returned to heaven. There they created many other gods and goddesses, including a sun-goddess called Amaterasu and a storm-god called Susanowo.

Amaterasu was a gentle, lovely goddess. She gave life to everything around her. But Susanowo was wild and fierce. He stormed around causing trouble.

One day Susanowo visited Amaterasu. He behaved so badly that she hid in a cave. The other gods and goddesses had to play a trick with a mirror to get her back out.

Another day Susanowo killed an eight-headed dragon who was about to eat a young girl. In the dragon's tail he found a sword. Susanowo gave the sword to Amaterasu to make up for his bad behavior. Then he married the girl he had saved.

Susanowo and his wife had many children. But none of them was good enough to rule Japan. So Amaterasu sent her grandson, Ninigi, to rule. She gave him three treasures to take with him. One was the mirror that had brought her from the cave. The second was a jewel from inside the cave. And the third was the sword from the dragon's tail.

This antique doll represents Jimmu Tenno, the first human emperor of Japan.

"Use these to rule Japan," said Amaterasu. "You and your descendants will rule forever."

Ninigi married and had three sons. One of them, Hoori, married the daughter of the sea-god. They had one son, who married and had four children. And one of those children was Jimmu Tenno, the great-great-great-grandson of the sun-goddess and the first human emperor of Japan.

That is the story told by legend. And, like many legends, it has its roots in truth. It is a fact that the Japanese imperial family is one of the oldest royal families in the world. The present emperor's ancestors go back to a time long before history was written down. The three treasures that Amaterasu supposedly gave her grandson are facts, too. The mirror and the sword are in two different shrines in Japan. The jewel is at the Imperial Palace in Tokyo. The Japanese call these treasures the Regalia. For centuries they have been the symbols of the imperial family's right to reign.

THE STORY TOLD BY HISTORY

The history of Japan goes back many hundreds of years. But it is hard to learn much about the early centuries because nothing was written down. Finally, in A.D. 712, the *Kojiki* (*Record of Ancient Things*) was written. In A.D. 720, someone wrote the *Nihongi* (*Chronicles of Japan*). Both of these, though, are mainly collections of myths and legends, such as the legend of Amaterasu.

For historical facts, scholars look at the histories of China and Korea. Sometimes these tell what was happening in Japan. Archaeological findings help, too. Together these sources tell us that the Japanese people originally came from many places—the mainland of Asia, southern China, the Philippines, and the South Pacific. This means that Japanese today are mostly a mixture of the Mongol and Malay people.

But one group of people lived in Japan long before these settlers arrived. They are called the Ainu. Scholars think the Ainu were very early members of the Caucasian race. As more and more newcomers arrived, the Ainu were pushed into northern Japan. Today about twenty thousand of them live in Japan, mostly on the island of Hokkaido.

During the first century A.D., many immigrants came to Japan by way of Korea. With them they brought long iron swords, special jewels carved into the shape of big commas, and bronze mirrors from China. These were the treasures that became the Regalia of the imperial family. But they were important in another way, too. They taught the Japanese to work with iron and bronze.

The early Japanese people lived together in clans (big groups of related families). These clans often fought to decide which would be the ruling clan. By A.D. 400, the Yamato clan was the most powerful. Its priest-chief became the leader of all the other clan chiefs. Its beliefs—including worship of a sun-goddess—became the beliefs of the other clans, too. And from the Yamatos, the first human emperor of Japan, Jimmu Tenno, is supposed to have come.

CHANGES FROM CHINA

Until the middle of the sixth century, most Japanese people followed the Shinto religion. It was a simple sort of nature worship. The sun, the moon, mountains, and even trees were gods.

Then, in 552, a missionary from southern Korea visited the Yamato clan. He officially introduced the Yamatos to the Buddhist religion. Buddhism had begun in India, but it soon spread to China and Korea. Now it was Japan's turn.

Priests came from China and Korea to teach the Japanese about Buddhism. Japanese people traveled to China to learn still more. And as they learned about the religion, they learned other things, too. They learned about Chinese philosophy, science, and the arts. Most important, they learned to write. Prince Shotoku, who ruled Japan from 593 until he died in 622, encouraged his people to learn all they could from the Chinese. Because of this, he is sometimes called "the founder of Japanese civilization."

Soon Japan began to think of itself as an empire (like China) instead of as a group of clans. Prince Shotoku even called himself the Emperor of the Rising Sun. (He called the emperor of China the Emperor of the Setting Sun.) But Shotoku also remained high priest of the Shinto religion. Some Japanese things would stay Japanese.

China also gave the Japanese new ideas about how to govern their country. In 645 a man named Kotoku became emperor. He decided that he should own all the land in Japan. He set up a complicated central government, a system of taxes, and a class of nobles at court. The time of Kotoku's rule is known as the Taika (Great Reform).

Toward the end of the eighth century, two more important changes happened in Japan's government. Until then, women had played a strong part. Some even had become empresses. But for centuries after that, there were no ruling empresses, although until the twelfth century, women had a rather high social position.

In 794 Emperor Kammu set up his capital in Heiankyo. (That's where the city of Kyoto stands today.) Suddenly a family called Fujiwara became important. They brought about the second big change. The Fujiwaras were clever, powerful people. Before long, they controlled the emperor and all the court nobles. Until 1160 they pretty well ruled the country—and did a good job, too. Everyone still *said* the emperor reigned. But the fact was that he had no power at all.

THE SHOGUNS

The Fujiwara family did much to develop literature and the arts in Japan. Under its leadership, many of the ideas borrowed from China were changed and made Japanese. (During this period, many famous works of literature were written by Japanese women.) But the Fujiwaras became so interested in these things that they forgot to run the country. Eventually they lost control of two important areas—politics and the economy.

While the people at court were writing poetry, some people out in the country were preparing to write a new chapter in Japan's history. These people were soldiers, descendants of the fierce clan chiefs. They had their own estates and defended them on horseback with their swords and bows. In many ways they were like the knights of Europe. The Japanese called them samurai.

Supposedly each samurai and his men owed allegiance to some noble family at court. But they didn't really care what was happening at court. They had enough to do defending their lands at home. Then the noble families began calling their samurai to the capital to help settle quarrels. That was a mistake.

Around 1160, the Taira family took control from the Fujiwaras. Twenty-five years later, the Minamotos defeated the Tairas. The leader of the Minamotos was a samurai called Yoritomo.

Yoritomo set up a military government. The emperor (who didn't have much choice) gave him a special title. He pronounced Yoritomo shogun (general). (The term shogun had been instituted a few centuries earlier. The shogun was important. Shogun has been more grandly translated as "Barbarian Quelling Generalissimo.") For the next seven hundred years shoguns controlled Japan. They ruled in the name of the emperor. But the ultimate power always was theirs.

Running the country was not easy for the shoguns. They had to fend off the other samurai families that wanted their power. In 1274 they ran into another problem. The Mongol leader Kublai Khan decided to invade Japan. When Mongolian forces attacked Japan, the shogun's samurai drove them back, and their ships were sunk by a typhoon (the name for hurricanes occurring in the

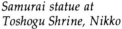
Samurai statue at Toshogu Shrine, Nikko

Pacific Ocean). In 1281 Kublai Khan tried again. Again a typhoon wiped out his fleet. The Japanese people called this typhoon *Kamikaze* ("divine wind").

In 1338 a new shogun family took over—the Ashikagas. They ruled for about 250 years. Then civil war brought a new shogun to power. He was a clever and ambitious leader named Toyotomi Hideyoshi. Hideyoshi wanted to build a great empire for Japan. He dreamed of ruling Korea and even China. His armies invaded Korea twice (in 1592 and 1597). But they failed to conquer Korea and never did get to China. Hideyoshi was shogun from 1585 to

1598. Because of his dream, he is sometimes called the Napoleon of Japan.

In 1603, one of Hideyoshi's lieutenants became shogun. He was from a different family—the Tokugawas. His family ruled Japan for more than 250 years.

EAST MEETS WEST

In the late 1200s, an Italian traveler named Marco Polo visited China. He went back to Europe with many wonderful tales. Some of them were about a land he called Cipango ("country where the sun rises"). Marco Polo didn't visit Cipango (Japan) himself. But the Chinese told him stories about it. They said it was a land full of gold and other treasures.

These tales of riches made other Europeans eager to get to Japan. In fact, Japan was one of the places Christopher Columbus hoped to find in 1492. But sailors from Portugal were the first Europeans to get there, in 1543. Before long they were trading with the Japanese. They also taught them to use firearms.

In 1549, a Roman Catholic priest, later canonized as St. Francis Xavier, went to Japan from Spain. He began to teach the Japanese about Christianity. Soon other missionaries from Spain and Portugal joined him. At first the Japanese welcomed them. Many Japanese became Christians.

Traders came with the missionaries, first from Spain and Portugal and then from England and The Netherlands. After a while the Japanese rulers worried that the Europeans might bring armies to conquer them. So, in 1614, they ordered all Christian priests to leave Japan and all Japanese to stop being Christians.

Commodore Matthew Perry landed in Japan on July 8, 1853.

Not everyone obeyed. In 1637, the Japanese army killed thousands of Japanese Christians. Then the government said all European traders must leave Japan, too. Only the Dutch could stay, because they didn't teach about Christianity.

Furthermore, the Japanese people were forbidden to leave their country. Those who were visiting other countries weren't allowed to come home. When foreign sailors were shipwrecked on a Japanese island, the Japanese killed them. Japan would have nothing to do with the rest of the world, said her rulers. And they stuck with this decision for over two hundred years.

But the government of the United States of America didn't like the way shipwrecked sailors were being treated. In 1853 Commodore Matthew C. Perry was sent to Japan with four warships. He asked the Japanese rulers for three things: diplomatic relations, trade relations, and humane treatment for American sailors. A year later Japan agreed.

Soon Great Britain, The Netherlands, and Russia asked for the same three things. Treaties were signed and, by 1858, Japan was part of the world community again.

When Emperor Meiji accepted a constitution in 1889, Japan became the first country in Asia to have a constitutional form of government.

BACK TO THE EMPEROR

Meanwhile, the Tokugawa family of shoguns was growing weaker. Its enemies began to call for a powerful emperor again. In 1867 the enemies won. Emperor Meiji proclaimed himself in charge, and his armies defeated the Tokugawas. The emperor moved his capital to the city of Edo and changed its named to Tokyo. Then he began making many other changes.

He set up a modern army and navy. He built schools and ordered Japanese children to attend them. He encouraged people to start businesses and industries. He changed the system of government and, in 1889, gave people their new constitution. "Learn all you can from the Europeans and Americans," he said.

Some things did not change. The Japanese still believed their emperor was the direct descendant of the sun-goddess. That meant he was divine. But in many other ways Japan was fast becoming a modern country.

Chapter 5

A LAND TO BE RECKONED WITH

BIRTH OF A WORLD POWER

By the end of the nineteenth century, Japan had grown into a powerful nation. Meanwhile, her neighbors, Korea and China, had grown weaker. The time is almost right, thought Japan's leaders, to start acting like a powerful nation. But there was one problem to be taken care of first.

That problem was the treaties Japan had signed with the Western powers. They gave the Western powers certain unfair rights and privileges. Foreigners could live in Japan without having to obey Japanese laws. Such a right is called extraterritoriality.

Japan wanted to be equal with the other powers in the world community. So, in 1880, she set up a new criminal code and, in 1890, a new civil code. Both codes gave foreigners fair treatment in Japanese courts. As soon as the foreign powers saw this, they were willing to change the treaties. Prince Hirobumi Ito was one of the Japanese leaders who worked hard to make all this happen.

In 1895 the Chinese and Japanese officials met to end the war between their two countries.

Now Japan could really start acting like a powerful nation. The first thing she did was to get involved in a war with China. This was in 1894/1895. Japan won. China had to give up control of Korea, the island of Taiwan, and the tip of Manchuria (called the Liaotung Peninsula). But Russia, Germany, and France made Japan give back the peninsula.

Relations between Japan and Russia began to worsen. In 1904 the Japanese declared war on Russia. For over a year both sides fought hard. Then U.S. President Theodore Roosevelt talked them into making peace. In 1905 Russia and Japan signed the Treaty of Portsmouth. The treaty agreed that Japan was in control of Korea. It gave the Liaotung Peninsula back to Japan, plus the South Manchurian Railway and the southern half of Sakhalin Island.

England had been Japan's ally during the war with Russia. When World War I broke out, the two countries remained friends. Japan immediately declared war on Germany, too. She didn't have

The Japanese fleet, under Admiral Togo (center), defeated the Russians in what is known as the Battle of the Japan Sea.

much to do with the war in Europe. But she did pounce on German possessions in Asia. These included the Mariana, Caroline, and Marshall islands in the North Pacific. Japan also took this opportunity to make some very strong demands upon China. These so-called "21 Demands" were intended to make China accept the control and protection of Japan. China refused these demands and went to Western powers to protest. Japan withdrew its demands for the time being.

European and American businessmen couldn't ship goods to Asia during the war. So Japanese businessmen began to manufacture and sell products formerly imported. Japanese business prospered as a result.

By the end of World War I, Japan was much richer and stronger than ever before. Acting like a world power had made her a world power. When a peace conference was held at Versailles in 1919, Japan was invited. She was officially one of the Big Five world powers now.

PEOPLE FOR PEACE

Ever since Emperor Meiji had defeated the Tokugawa family in the late 1860s, Japan had been run by a small group of strong leaders. They were responsible for making Japan a world power. But after World War I, they began to lose some of their popularity.

The Japanese people began picking up new ideas everywhere. They read books from the West. They listened to Christian missionaries, mostly from the United States. Not many of them became Christians, but they learned a lot about Western beliefs. Businessmen watched how Western businesses operated. And everyone noticed that the more democratic countries had won World War I. Maybe Japan should become more democratic, too.

Political parties became more and more important in the government. They forced the leaders to do what they wanted. And some of the most powerful people in the political parties were businessmen. After all, they had done a lot for Japan during the war. It looked as if they could do a lot for her in the future, too.

The businessmen didn't think war was the best way to get rich. They didn't want to pay taxes to support a big army and navy. They would rather trade with other countries than fight them. The people were ready to listen to the businessmen.

Japan became an original member of the League of Nations in 1920. She agreed with other world powers to reduce the size of her navy. She gave back some of the area she had won in China. She signed the Nine-Power Treaty, which guaranteed China's independence. She signed the Kellogg Peace Treaty, which said war was no way to settle quarrels. She signed the London Naval Treaty, which limited her navy even more. All at once, Japan, a nation of fierce warriors, had become a nation eager for peace.

PEOPLE FOR WAR

But not every Japanese was eager for peace. Most of the people who wanted peace lived in the cities and understood Western ideas. People from the countryside and small villages raised their eyebrows at all this. Japan, they thought, should stick with Japanese ideas.

Many military people felt the same way. Japan had become a world power by going to war. If she wanted to stay one, she had better continue going to war.

The country people and the military soon became close allies. Not only did they feel the same about peace and war, but country people also saw the army as their only chance for a better life.

Secret societies began popping up. Some of them spread hate-filled propaganda and used terrorist tactics. One of the best known was a group that hated Russians and wanted Japan to take control of Russian land in Siberia. They were called the Amur (Black Dragon) Society.

Then, around 1930, Japan began to feel the effects of the Great Depression that was sweeping world economies. Foreign powers weren't sending her raw materials anymore. They weren't buying the things Japan made. Suddenly businessmen began to lose their influence. More and more people started paying attention to the military instead.

In 1931, a bomb exploded on the South Manchurian Railway. The military said the Chinese had set it off. They urged a takeover of Manchuria as the only way to protect the railway. The Japanese government didn't approve, but couldn't stop the military. By 1932, Japan had conquered all of Manchuria. Its name was changed to Manchukuo.

The League of Nations protested. So did the United States. Japan simply quit the League. Winning the war in Manchuria had helped the Japanese economy. So the military must have been right all along—even the businessmen were saying so now. Besides, they were making money again.

The power of military leaders in the government increased. In 1937 they began a war against China. By the end of 1938, they had won a lot of Chinese territory, including some important cities.

The Japanese also signed anti-Communist treaties with Germany and Italy. They sank a U.S. gunboat in China. (They did apologize for this, though, and paid damages to the United States.) They fought with Russian soldiers on the Manchurian-Siberian border. As the storm clouds of World War II gathered, it was clear which side Japan would be on.

WAR

In September, 1939, World War II began in Europe. In 1940, Germany invaded France, so Japan invaded French Indochina. By 1941, Japan was totally at war. General Hideki Tojo became prime minister. Now the military had full control of the government.

Japan was already unhappy with the United States. In 1940, the United States had cut down on the oil and scrap iron she was selling to Japan. Japanese leaders thought American people were weak. They had too many luxuries. They had never fought a long, hard war. So, on December 7, 1941, Japan attacked U.S. military bases at Pearl Harbor in Hawaii. She also attacked Guam, Midway, and the Philippine Islands. She almost wiped out the U.S. Navy. And, for a while, she went on winning one battle after another in the Pacific.

Tourists from many countries visit the Arizona Memorial in Pearl Harbor, Hawaii.

But Japan had made one bad mistake. Before Pearl Harbor, many American people didn't want to get involved in another world war. Pearl Harbor changed their minds fast. They went right to work rebuilding their navy and putting together a first-class army and air force.

In 1942, Japan lost battles at Midway and Guadalcanal. She was tired after years of war. The United States, on the other hand, was fresh—and angry. Japan's servicemen fought with bravery. But bravery wasn't enough and they went on losing.

By 1945, the United States was attacking the Japanese homeland. Planes, submarines, and warships worked together to cut off her supplies and destroy her factories. On August 6, the United States dropped an atomic bomb on the city of Hiroshima. This was the first atomic bomb ever used in a war. On August 8, Russia invaded Manchuria and Korea. And, on August 9, the United States dropped an even bigger atomic bomb on the city of Nagasaki.

On August 15, Emperor Hirohito told the Japanese people they were going to surrender. The formal surrender ceremony came on September 2 on the U.S. battleship *Missouri*. Japan had lost all of her possessions on mainland Asia and all of her islands in the Pacific. All she had left were her four main islands and some little ones nearby. The nation was in ruins. Millions of people were dead.

OCCUPIED

For the first time in history, Japan found herself under the control of foreign conquerers. General Douglas MacArthur of the U.S. Army was appointed Supreme Commander for the Allied Powers. He gave the orders and the Japanese government carried them out. MacArthur had two goals: to dismantle Japan's military power and to make Japan's government more democratic and peaceful. He also had thousands of U.S. troops to help him reach his goals.

The years of occupation could have been a horrible time for the Japanese people, but they weren't. For the most part, the Americans were sensible and friendly. And so were the Japanese. Soon Japan had a new constitution. It went into effect on May 3,

General Douglas MacArthur and Emperor Hirohito

1947. Constitution Day is still an important holiday in Japan.

The new constitution took away all the emperor's political power. It got rid of the ruling class of nobles. It gave women the right to vote. It abolished the army and navy. It said that Japan could not use war as a political weapon anymore.

Japan's economic system changed, too. Now farmers could own their own land. Workers could belong to labor unions. The old, enormous industrial combines (called *zaibatsu*) were wiped out. This huge business organization whose influence and production had done so much for Japan's war effort was broken down into much smaller, separate businesses.

In 1951, Japan signed a peace treaty with forty-eight other countries. (Russia and Communist China didn't sign.) This treaty went into effect on April 28, 1952. The occupation of Japan was officially over.

CHANGES AND MORE CHANGES

Japan faced many serious problems after the war. Half of the houses in her cities were destroyed. In Tokyo, half the population had died. Other cities also had suffered great losses. Japan had no ships to transport her goods. She didn't have enough food to feed her people. Her economy was in shambles.

The Americans tried to help Japan solve these problems. But most of the hard work was done by the Japanese themselves. They learned new ways of farming. They built shacks to house people for the time being. Then they built skyscrapers. Workers labored hard. Technicians learned new technologies. And industries boomed.

Japan had new goals now—international trade and world peace. In 1952 she tried to join the United Nations. Russia said no. But in 1956 Russia and Japan signed their own treaty. Then Russia let her into the United Nations.

Japan's government changed, too. It is now divided into three branches—executive, legislative, and judicial. The legislative branch is the strongest. It is called the Diet and is like a parliament.

There are two houses in the Diet. Voters elect the 511 members of the House of Representatives for four-year terms. They elect the 252 members of the House of Councillors for six-year terms. The Diet chooses one of its members to be prime minister. He is head of the executive branch and chooses the cabinet. But half of the cabinet members must be from the Diet.

The judicial branch of government is divided into a Supreme Court, eight regional high courts, fifty district courts, and many summary and family courts.

The 1964 Olympics (left) were held in Tokyo. The Diet, the legislative branch of the government, meets in this building (right).

Japan itself is divided into forty-seven prefectures. They are somewhat like states in the United States. Each prefecture chooses a governor and an assembly. Each city, town, and village chooses a mayor and a local assembly.

The emperor of Japan is no longer considered divine. Instead, he is called a "symbol of the state and of the unity of the people." The constitution says that. It also says quite clearly that all power belongs to the people.

Japan adjusted quickly to the new government and watched still more changes come along, one after another. Crown Prince Akihito married a commoner. No crown prince had done *that* before. Emperor Hirohito and Empress Nagako traveled to Europe. No reigning emperor had done *that* before. The 1964 Summer Olympics took place in Tokyo. No Olympics had ever even been held in Asia before.

Japanese grocery store

Japan still has problems. She depends on other nations for many of her needs. The world oil shortage in the 1970s hit her hard. Environmental pollution is another problem for a country with so much industry. Inflation troubles her just as it does other countries. Her complicated language sometimes makes trade and diplomatic relationships with other peoples more difficult.

But Japan has shown the world that she can solve her problems. In a little over a hundred years, she has grown from an isolated country to a useful member of the world community. She has learned much from the West. But she hasn't given up the best of her past. Now no one is asking, "Will Japan make it?" Instead they ask, "What on earth will Japan manage to do next?"

Chapter 6

MAKERS OF JAPAN

THE HISTORY MAKERS

Some people are remembered because of their great deeds. Because of them, people born many years later live different lives than they would have otherwise. Such doers of deeds are the people who make a nation's history.

The first such person in Japan's history was a man called Jimmu Tenno. Legend says he was the great-great-great-grandson of the sun-goddess Amaterasu. He led his warriors from the island of Kyushu to Yamato (an area on the island of Honshu around Osaka and Nara). There, in 660 B.C., he became emperor and direct ancestor of all the emperors to come.

Historians know that a group of people did come from the south. They did establish a powerful clan in the Yamato area. Historians think all this happened later than 660 B.C. But, in some way, Jimmu Tenno must have existed. Maybe he was one man. Maybe he was a group of people. In either case, his deeds are remembered and so is he.

Much later, a man known as Prince Shotoku gave Japan's history a strong twist in a new direction. Shotoku ruled as regent

Illustration of thirteen-year-old Yoritomo going into battle for the first time.

for his aunt, Empress Suiko, from A.D. 593 to 622. He had studied Buddhism and Chinese culture and was eager to share his learning. First he drew up a code called the Seventeen Article Constitution. It was based on Chinese theories of government. Shotoku's constitution stated clearly which responsibilities and powers belonged to the ruler and which to the people. It was Japan's first written theory of government.

Shotoku also encouraged his people to imitate Chinese literature, art, and music. He adopted the Chinese calendar for them. For all these reasons, he is known as "the founder of Japanese civilization."

Hundreds of years passed. Emperors and empresses came and went. Special warriors, known as samurai, grew in power. Finally, in the late 1100s, one of them took over the government. He was from the Minamoto family and his name was Yoritomo. The emperor gave him the title of shogun (general). So Minamoto

Yoritomo had the most powerful position in Japan. But it was his younger half brother, Minamoto Yoshitsune, who won the battles for him. And it is Yoshitsune who has lived in the hearts of the Japanese people ever since.

Yoshitsune had been brought up to be a monk. But that wasn't what he wanted. So he ran away from the monastery and went north. There, and in Kyoto, he learned military arts. He also made friends with other warriors, who agreed to follow and fight with him.

When Yoshitsune was ready, he asked Yoritomo to let him fight for him. Yoritomo agreed and Yoshitsune won the battles that made Yoritomo the shogun. Then Yoritomo became worried. He didn't realize how loyal Yoshitsune was. He thought his brother might try to steal his power. After many attempts, he managed to trap Yoshitsune. Rather than be killed by his enemies, Yoshitsune killed himself in the honorable samurai way. But his story lives on. It has inspired many Japanese people to acts of bravery, loyalty, and honor.

More centuries flowed past, bringing many dark times for the Japanese. Kublai Khan attacked and was turned away by the *Kamikaze* ("divine wind"). Civil wars erupted one after another. Then came three men who leaped into Japanese history and once more changed its course.

One was Oda Nobunaga, a powerful young daimyo (lord) who was born in 1534. Nobunaga couldn't be a shogun himself. He came from the wrong family. But he set up a man called Ashikaga Yoshiaki as shogun. Then he ran things from behind the scenes. Finally he got rid of Yoshiaki, too.

Nobunaga was a violent man. He couldn't get along with anyone, neither his parents nor the monks they sent him to. But

*Collection of
Japanese swords*

Nobunaga had the support of two powerful friends. One was a
general called Toyotomi Hideyoshi. The other was a relative by
marriage called Tokugawa Ieyasu. Hideyoshi truly respected
Nobunaga and wanted only to serve him as a soldier. Ieyasu had
been part of a group Nobunaga defeated. He decided he wanted to
serve this powerful man. So he married his son to Nobunaga's
niece and joined his new relative's forces.

Together the three men put down group after group who were
hungry for power in Japan. Then another of Nobunaga's generals
turned traitor. Nobunaga was forced to kill himself rather than be
killed by this man. The traitor, Mitsuhide, tried to take over the
government. But his victory lasted only thirteen days. Then
Hideyoshi had him killed.

Now Hideyoshi was in charge. He trampled down the rest of
his enemies and Japan was finally at peace. Hideyoshi made many
rigid laws that took away the people's freedom. But their lives
were easier, too. Hideyoshi's big mistake came when he decided to
invade Korea and China. Twice. He lost. Both times. But because
of his big dreams, he is known as the Napoleon of Japan.

Five years after Hideyoshi died, Ieyasu became shogun. He made all Christian missionaries leave Japan. He also divided the Japanese people into classes. Each class had to follow strict rules. Ieyasu even told them what they could and couldn't wear. Ieyasu's family ruled Japan for more than 250 years.

Nobunaga, Hideyoshi, and Ieyasu were all tough, harsh men. But together they did Japan a great favor. They changed her from a country torn by civil wars to a unified nation. Hideyoshi and Ieyasu also cut her off from the rest of the world. This gave Japan a chance to grow and become a strong nation.

By the middle of the 1800s, Ieyasu's family, the Tokugawas, had grown weak. At the same time, nations such as the United States began urging Japan to join the rest of the world community. It was time for a strong, new leader. In 1867 the shogun was defeated by those who supported the emperor's rule. Emperor Meiji became the actual leader of the nation.

"I am the emperor," he said. "All power belongs to me. There will be no more shoguns." He proved this by having his armies crush the rest of the Tokugawa forces.

Emperor Meiji moved the capital to Edo and changed its name to Tokyo. He made many other changes, too. He got rid of the samurai class of warriors and set up a modern army and navy. He made reforms in the government, education, and the economy. Above all, he encouraged Japan to learn all she could from the West.

The Emperor abolished much of the old class system, but he retained some privileges. Former feudal lords and those who did distinguished services to the state were called nobles and given special privileges. The emperor also encouraged the people to go on believing he was divine.

Eventually Emperor Meiji used all these ideas—the new Western ones and the old Japanese ones—to make his country very powerful indeed. Then he led her into wars with China and Russia. In both cases Japan won.

Emperor Meiji died in 1912. He had ruled Japan for forty-five years. He had been smart enough to surround himself with many good assistants. But much of Japan's growth during this period was due to no one but the emperor himself.

THE BEAUTY MAKERS

Some people are remembered because of the beautiful things they have created. Such people capture their own feelings and the spirit of an age in words or music or paint or film. Because of them, others in their own age and later ages better understand the beauty and meaning of their lives. They are a nation's artists.

One such person who appeared early in Japan's history was the poet Kakinomoto-no-Hitomaro. Hitomaro lived from about 655 to about 709. He was probably a poet laureate (official poet) for the imperial court. Many of Hitomaro's poems tell about trips taken by the people of the court or about famous people who died. Sometimes he also wrote about the death of times gone by. But Hitomaro's most beautiful and moving poems are about the death of his wife.

Many of Hitomaro's poems are included in the *Manyoshu* (*Collection of Ten Thousand Leaves*). This is a giant anthology of Japanese poetry, mostly from the seventh and eighth centuries.

Women played an extremely important part in the development of Japanese literature. For years men wouldn't write in Japanese. They felt it was better to write in Chinese characters and copy the ideas of Chinese writers. Most of their work was no better than any imitation ever is. But Japanese women wrote in Japanese syllabary called *kana.* In this way they both helped develop their language and spoke their thoughts in fresh new ways.

One form in which Japanese women often wrote was called the *nikki.* A *nikki* is sort of a combination diary, journal, and collection of memories. Usually the wives and daughters of noblemen wrote *nikki.* They told about events in their daily lives, their feelings, and their love affairs.

One of the first writers of a *nikki* was a woman who was the mother of Fujiwara Michitsuna, the Minister of the Right in the Fujiwara period. She lived in the tenth century and was the wife of a man named Jujiwara-no-Kaneie. Her *nikki* was called *Kagero nikki* (*Gossamer Diary*). In it she spoke about her own life.

A woman named Sei Shonagon wrote another important book during this period. It is called *Makura no soshi* (*The Pillow Book*). Sei Shonagon was a noblewoman who lived at the imperial court. Her book includes little stories about events at court and her impressions of what was going on. It's a lively book and sometimes a funny one.

Back in the ninth century, the Japanese already were writing books that are a lot like the novels of today. These books were called *monogatari.* The most famous, *Genji monogatari* (*The Tale of Genji*), was written early in the eleventh century by a woman known as Lady Murasaki Shikibu. Lady Murasaki was born about 974 and died about 1031. She was the wife of a nobleman and lady-in-waiting to Empress Akiko. Murasaki was probably a nickname. Shikibu was her father's title. (He was also a nobleman.) So we don't even know her real name. But we do know she was one of Japan's greatest writers.

Mount Sakurajima, Red, *1935 painting by Umehara Ryuzaburo,*
combines influence of Western art with traditional Japanese painting.

Around 1010, Lady Murasaki wrote a *nikki* (*Murasaki Shikibu
nikki*), as did so many other women. But it was *The Tale of Genji*
that won her lasting fame. This huge novel (over one thousand
pages long) tells about the life, adventures, and loves of Prince
Genji, supposedly the son of an emperor and his concubine.

Not all of Japan's great artists were writers. She also has had her
share of famous painters. One of the best known was Katsushika
Hokusai (1760-1849). He was born in Edo (Tokyo) and taught
himself to paint and work with color prints. Some of his works
are *Thirty-Six Views of Fuji, Hundred Views of Fuji,* and *Famous
Bridges and Waterfalls.* Hokusai's prints were exhibited in Europe
where they influenced many European artists. But Hokusai never
earned much money and lived in poverty.

In recent times, Japan has also been working with film. Akira
Kurosawa was the first Japanese director to become
internationally famous. He was born in Tokyo in 1910. Some of
his best-known films include *Rashomon, Ikiru, I Live in Fear,* and
Seven Samurai.

Chapter 7

LIVING IN THE LAND

THE RESOURCE THAT CAN'T BE BEAT

Japan has very few mineral resources. She has to import iron, oil, copper, zinc, bauxite, lead, potassium salts, phosphate rock, and salt. She has some coal, but only one third of her needs. So she imports a lot of coal, too.

Japan has little land to use for farming. Because of her many mountains, only about 15 percent of her total land can be used for crops.

Both of these shortages—mineral resources and farmland—can be serious problems for any nation. But Japan has gone a long way to solving both of them. That's because she has one resource that can't be beat—her people.

The Japanese people are well educated. Surveys show that 99.3 percent of them can read and write. They are always ready to learn new information and new techniques. And they don't mind working hard. Most Japanese people feel a strong sense of loyalty to their jobs.

In a little over a hundred years, Japan has grown from an isolated nation to one of the leading industrial powers of the world. Her people enjoy a high standard of living. Many can afford some luxuries as well as the things they need. Other countries are eager to import things made in Japan. They know they're good. Most of the credit for all this belongs to Japan's greatest resource—her people.

A WORKSHOP FOR THE WORLD

First Japan must import the raw materials she needs. Then she makes them into goods and sells them to other countries. This makes her a sort of workshop for the world. More than one fourth of her workers are involved in manufacturing.

Some of the goods Japan produces include iron and steel, ships, locomotives, automobiles, railroad cars, heavy machinery, electronic equipment, chemicals, textiles, raw silk, paper, precision tools, cameras, lenses, and handicraft articles.

To find out where most of Japan's factories are, draw an imaginary line on the map from Nagasaki to Tokyo. Most of the industrial centers lie near this line. The Osaka-Kobe-Kyoto area is important for cotton textiles and ships. The Nagasaki-Kitakyushu area concentrates on pig iron, steel, cement, ships, glass, and chemicals. Nagoya and the Tokyo-Yokohama area are also industrial centers.

In general, Japanese companies treat their workers well. They offer many benefits, such as cash bonuses, inexpensive housing, company stores, medical and hospital care, and recreational facilities. Many even guarantee that their workers have jobs for life.

But Japanese industry still has problems to solve. Most businesses require workers to retire at age fifty-five, but these people receive pensions from their companies for the rest of their lives, in addition to their social security benefits. Finally, it's not always wise to depend on other countries to supply raw materials and buy finished products. World politics and economic trends can cause industrial disasters.

The Japanese are working on these problems, though. They've solved some tough ones in the past. No doubt they'll solve these, too.

A LOT WITH A LITTLE

There are over 118 million people in Japan. Farmers have only 15 percent of the total land for crops. Yet they raise close to three fourths of all the food that is needed by all of those people. That's doing a lot with a little!

One sixth of Japan's workers are farmers. Ninety percent of the farms are worked by their owners. That wasn't true before World War II. Back then there were many tenant farmers. But after the war Japan began making some important land reforms.

The use of farm machinery and chemicals was another big change that took place after World War II. Before the war, farmers did almost everything by hand. Now their job is a lot easier and their farms are a lot more efficient. Even though the average farm is only about 2.4 acres (1 hectare) in size, most farmers earn a good living. Many also have time to hold extra jobs in nearby cities and towns.

The most important crop raised in Japan is rice. Rice is grown in paddies, which are flooded fields with dikes or dirt walls around

To utilize the land fully Japanese farmers cut terraces in the hillsides.
Rice is grown on many hillsides (left). Tea leaves are picked by hand.

them. Japanese rice-growers have become very clever at carving rice paddies out of hillsides. This technique is called terracing. It gives the growers more land to work with.

Other important crops include barley, cabbages, fruits, onions, potatoes, radishes, wheat, soybeans, and tea. Tea is a favorite drink in Japan. Tea leaves grow on bushes and the bushes grow well on hillsides. So Japan is able to supply herself with all the tea she can drink.

Japan doesn't raise as many farm animals as do many other countries. That's because animals need a lot of room and a lot of grain to eat. The farmers who do raise animals often choose smaller ones, such as pigs and chickens. Only on Hokkaido is there room for many cattle. Most of Japan's dairy products come from this northern island.

Cuttlefish are dried in the sun at Ajiro Port.

TREASURES FROM THE SEA

Fishing has always been important in Japan and still is. Fish are the main source of protein for Japanese people. But they also export a lot of frozen, fried, and canned fish to other countries.

Japan has over 449,000 fishing vessels. That's more than any other country in the world has. Some of these vessels are owned by private fishermen who live in little villages near the sea. But many belong to big companies. These company ships travel all over the Pacific Ocean. Some have canning machinery right on board.

Japanese fishermen bring in almost 12 million short tons (10,886,400 metric tonnes) of fish each year. These include salmon, tuna, shellfish, and many other kinds.

In the 1920s, the Japanese figured out a way to make oysters in cages produce pearls. These are called cultured pearls. They're another important export for Japan—and another treasure from the sea.

High-speed electric trains, often called bullet trains, connect one end of Honshu with the other.

SOMETHING FOR EVERYONE

Of course, there are many other kinds of jobs in Japan. Some people work in service professions, such as medicine, law, and education. Some work in the arts and literature. Some play professional sports.

The communications area also employs many people. Telephone, telegraph, and postal services are run by the government. Radio and television are extremely popular. More than 98 percent of all Japanese families own a color TV. Newspaper circulation in Japan is third highest in the world, exceeded by only Russia and the United States.

Then there are the people whose job it is to get other people to work—or play. It wasn't easy to build railroads in Japan. All those

A supertanker slides into the water. Japan leads the world in shipbuilding.

mountains got in the way. But the Japanese kept at it. Today most of them travel by train. The government owns and runs most of the railroads.

Two out of five families in Japan own a car. In some areas traffic is a nightmare and many roads need improving. That's why many people prefer the bus or subway.

All the major cities in Japan have airports and they are heavily used. In fact, Osaka and Tokyo have the busiest airports in all of Asia.

But an island nation is bound to depend greatly on ships. The Japanese people certainly do. They have the second largest merchant fleet in the world. And that means still more jobs for still more people.

Illustration by Katsushika Hokusai (1760-1849) of a poem by Sanji Hitoshi

Chapter 8

VOICES OF THE LAND

CREATED IN JAPAN

Japanese arts, crafts, and literature have a long history. Sometimes they were heavily influenced by other cultures. In the past, Chinese influence was important. Today it is the influence of the West.

But much art in Japan is closely tied to her religious thought, both Buddhist and Shinto. And, no matter how great the foreign influence, Japanese creations always seem to remain very much themselves and very much Japanese.

BRUSH, PAINT, AND WOOD

Japanese artists learned to paint from the Chinese. At the same time they were learning about Buddhism. So, many early paintings show religious subjects. Around 1100, artists began painting on scrolls. Their brightly colored pictures told stories about Japan and weren't at all like Chinese pictures.

Then, about 1300, Chinese influence returned. The scrolls became mainly landscape paintings in black only. But by the late 1500s, China was out again. Japanese subjects with bright colors were back in.

Satin theatrical over-robe embroidered in colored silks and cotton is adorned with gold-wrapped thread and glass beads.

During the 1600s, Japanese bankers and merchants urged artists to paint only pictures of everyday life in Japan. They bought so many of these pictures that artists began printing them. They used carved wooden blocks to make their prints.

Wood-block printing is still important in Japan. Two famous artists in the field are Katsushika Hokusai and Hiroshige Ando. They lived in the 1800s. Umetaro Azechi is a modern wood-block printer. Painting on paper screens is also a special art in Japan.

From the 600s to the 1300s, Japanese artists created some fine sculpture. Most of their statues were of Buddha. Many of them still can be seen in temples. Most are made of wood. But some artists used bronze or clay.

A COUNTRY OF CRAFTSPEOPLE

Japan is a country rich in crafts. In one village people may be making round, red Daruma dolls, which bounce back up when they are knocked over. (These dolls say something important about the Japanese people.) In Kyoto graceful dancing dolls are dressed in silk kimonos. Japanese dolls such as these meant to be looked at rather than played with.

In another village busy workers have created a flock of gorgeous kites—butterflies, fish, and dragons—just waiting to fly away. In yet another, people make lacquer boxes, tables, chests, and trays. Some of these bright red or black objects have received forty coats of lacquer. Their surfaces are as smooth as silk.

Silk weaving is another important craft in Japan. So is the making of pottery and porcelain. Much beautiful cloisonné comes from Japan. Cloisonné is a special technique of painting small objects and jewelry with bright enamels.

Japan's craftspeople make so many beautiful things that crafts are one of Japan's chief exports to the rest of the world.

SHAMISENS AND SAXOPHONES

East and West really do meet in Japanese music. At certain theaters and festivals, traditional Japanese music is played. It originally came from China and India and sounds strange to those who have not heard it before. Traditional instruments include the *fue* (woodwind instrument), *shakuhachi* (a sort of flute), the *koto* (a harp, stringed instrument), the *biwa* (something like a mandolin), the *shamisen* (something like a banjo), the *taiko* (a large wooden drum that resembles a brass drum although it comes in many sizes), gongs, cymbals, and hand drums.

But many concert halls present Western music, such as a symphony, a Puccini opera, or jazz. Tokyo itself has seven symphony orchestras. The Japanese have developed some excellent ways of teaching young children to play musical instruments. These children grow up and find jobs in first-rate orchestras all over the world.

Popular music of the West is just as popular in Japan. It's heard in nightclubs, cabarets, discos, and concert halls. Visitors may stop in their tracks the first time they hear a favorite song sung in Japanese.

Some contemporary Japanese composers are trying to combine the sounds of traditional Japanese music with modern techniques of composition. The results sound very different—and often very pleasant.

FROM NO TO A SHOOT-OUT

Japan is best known for two forms of drama—No plays and Kabuki. No plays were first performed in the 1300s. They were designed for upper-class audiences. Everything about them is

Guitarist (left) represents the new trends in Japanese society, while the Kabuki players symbolize the country's traditional heritage.

formal and dignified. All of the actors wear masks and a chorus chants most of the story. In the background, musicians play drums and a flute.

Kabuki plays, on the other hand, are livelier and easier to understand. They were developed in the 1500s for ordinary audiences. Actors wear heavy makeup instead of masks. The way they sing, dance, and speak may seem overly dramatic and startling to a Western viewer. The musical background for Kabuki plays is provided by drums, cymbals, flutes, gongs, *shamisens*, and those wooden blocks that get banged on the floor.

Japanese people also enjoy Western plays, movies, and television. They produce hundreds of films each year, including science-fiction thrillers and even versions of American westerns.

THE TELLERS OF STORIES

The rest of the world didn't know much about Japanese literature before the 1900s. Then it found out what it was missing. Now Japanese literature is considered to be among the greatest in the world.

The two oldest works are the *Kojiki* (*Record of Ancient Things*) and the *Nihongi* (*Chronicles of Japan*). They were written in the 700s, and contain many stories, myths, legends, and songs.

The greatest work of Japanese fiction, *The Tale of Genji,* was written early in the 1000s. The author of this long novel was Murasaki Shikibu, lady-in-waiting to the empress. Her story tells many details about court life.

During the 1600s, a form of short, nonrhyming poetry developed that is still popular in Japan. It's called haiku and it always contains exactly seventeen syllables printed in three lines. Three famous writers of haiku were Basho, Buson, and Issa. Here is a translation of one of Basho's haiku:

> The old pond
> A frog jumps in
> The sound of the water.

Many modern Japanese authors write novels. In 1968 Yasunari Kawabata won the Nobel Prize in literature. Two of his best-known works are *Snow Country* and *A Thousand Cranes*. Both have been translated into English.

ISLANDS OF PEACE

Japan is a busy, crowded country. How do her people keep from feeling crushed by all that is going on around them? They have

Peaceful gardens, and simple, but elegant, flower arrangements reflect the Japanese love of nature.

held on to two things—their traditions and their love of nature. These have helped the Japanese create peaceful little islands in the middle of their busy lives.

Their gardens are one example of these islands. They're usually simple with a few trees, rocks, flowers, and some water. Their very simplicity makes them peaceful places in which to sit and forget the noisy world.

Traditional Japanese architecture also gives a feeling of peacefulness. It tries to blend in with nature. Buildings are usually wooden and unpainted. Sliding doors separate the rooms. Other sliding doors open out onto gardens. Roofs of blue gray tiles blend in quietly with the sky.

Even flower arranging (called "ikebana" in Japanese) follows traditional rules and tries to blend in with nature. You won't see many large, bright bouquets. Instead, a few flowers and some twigs are carefully arranged to look as if they're still growing. The result? A very peaceful, elegant flower arrangement.

Chapter 9

THE LAND

AND THE PEOPLE

A HAPPY MIXTURE

A Japanese visitor to the United States went with a friend to a Japanese festival in a large midwestern city.

"I almost didn't ask you to go," said her friend later. "I thought you could see all those things at home."

"Oh, no!" said the Japanese girl. "Why, some of them I've never seen before. That festival was more Japanese than Japan."

Life in Japan is changing very quickly. It's becoming more Western. Most Japanese people now wear Western clothes except for special occasions or for relaxing at home. Then they might slip into a *yukata*. That's a long, loose cotton robe, made with flowing sleeves, tied at the waist with a sash called an *obi*. But young people often skip the *yukata* and just wear jeans.

In the past, Japanese parents usually decided whom their children would marry. That doesn't happen too often anymore. But most Japanese young people do wait until they're eighteen to date. And Japanese parents still influence either directly or indirectly their child's choice of a marriage partner.

Women's lives were much more sheltered in Japan before World War II. Most of them stayed at home most of the time. Now Japanese women are free to hold jobs and take part in political and social organizations. And many of them do.

Yes, life in Japan is changing very quickly. But the Japanese people aren't changing just for the sake of doing something different. They're careful to change only when change will make life better in some way. They're also holding on to some important parts of their past.

For example, they're holding on to their courtesy. (That's especially important in such a crowded country.) Japanese people are polite to one another. They do all they can to make visitors feel welcome. They show great respect for their elders. And the Japanese never embarrass anyone in front of other people if they can help it.

The Japanese also are holding on to some of the virtues that have been important throughout their history. They admire bravery. They try to be honorable in all facets of their lives. They are loyal to their friends, families, jobs, and country. They believe in hard work.

Finally, the Japanese are holding on to their love for certain things. One of these is children. The Japanese even have special days set aside each year to honor their children. They love beauty, too, especially the beauty of nature. They show this love in their buildings (even the modern ones), their gardens, the things they like to do on holidays and vacations, and in many other ways.

Despite the changes since World War II, the Japanese people have not given up the good things from their past. Instead, they have chosen a happy mixture of old and new, East and West.

Students learn to draw characters using a brush. There are thousands of characters in the Japanese language.

A LOT TO LEARN

In a land where hard work and progress are so important, education is important, too. Almost all the Japanese people can read and write. And the Japanese language isn't easy.

First, there are several forms of spoken Japanese. Three of these are the intimate, the polite, and the honorific. The intimate is used at home. The polite is for speaking in well-educated company. The honorific shows respect for older people or superiors. (For a Westerner trying to handle all this, there's something else to remember. In Japan, a person's family name is given first. So your name might be Jones Bob.)

There are different ways of writing Japanese. One uses *kanji*. *Kanji* are symbols that stand for whole words. The Japanese borrowed their *kanji* from the Chinese during the 500s. Before that, the Japanese language couldn't be written. The other way of writing uses symbols that stand for sounds, not words. They're called *kana*. *Kana* are put together to make words.

All in all, hundreds of *kanji* and *kana* must be memorized in order to read and write Japanese. (It's even more complicated, but that gives the general idea.) Japanese children also learn to write their language in the Roman alphabet.

Nine years of school are required for Japanese children. During this time they have a great deal of homework, including special assignments in the summer. After six years of elementary school and three years of junior high, they take a special examination. If they pass, they can go on to senior high for three years.

Students who want to attend college must take another examination. Those who pass go to one of over one thousand colleges and universities in Japan.

POWERFUL FORCES

Religion has always played an important part in Japanese life. At first, most Japanese followed the Shinto religion. (Shinto means "the ways of the gods.") Shinto teaches that mountains, the sea, trees, and other forms of nature are divine. It is a kind of nature worship. Eventually the Japanese added ancestor worship to their Shinto beliefs. In 1870, when Shinto was proclaimed the state religion of Japan, the emperor was considered divine, too.

After World War II, Shinto was no longer the state religion. Emperor Hirohito announced he was no longer divine. But many people still believe in other parts of Shinto. More than 80,000 Shinto shrines and 75,000 Buddhist temples are spread throughout the country. And Shinto has had a great influence on

*Burning incense
at Kyoto Temple*

the way Japanese people think, especially their feelings toward
older people, traditions, and nature.

Buddhism came to Japan from China and Korea in 552. Today
there are four Buddhist sects in Japan: *Zen, Jodo, Shin,* and
Nichiren. Since many people who follow Buddhism also follow
Shinto, it's hard to say how the two religions compare in size. But
Buddhism has also influenced life in Japan, especially its art.

Christianity arrived in Japan much later than Buddhism.
Spanish and Portuguese missionaries first introduced it in the
1500s. Then, for over two hundred years, it was banned. Today
there are about 900,000 Japanese Christians and about three
thousand churches.

A new religious organization developed in Japan after World
War II. It's called *Soka Gakkai* (Value Creation Academy). *Soka
Gakkai* is a form of Buddhism. Its followers are especially active in
Japanese political life.

Tatami-covered floor and sliding doors that lead to a garden are features of a traditional Japanese home. In modern apartments, however, the interiors will be furnished in the Western style, including TVs, stereos, and radios.

STRAW MATS AND ATARI

What are Japanese homes like? That depends on what sort of home you visit. In rural areas people usually live in one- or two-story houses. Older ones may be made of wood with thatched or tiled roofs. Newer ones may be made of cement blocks with tiled roofs. In cities most people live in their own houses or apartments.

Many homes in Japan still are arranged in the traditional way. Straw mats (call tatami) cover the floors. Japanese people usually wear slippers when they walk on corridors not covered with tatami, but they take off the slippers upon entering tatami-covered rooms. They sit on cushions on the floor and eat from low tables. When it is time for bed, they spread out quilts on the floors. Newer homes, however, often have at least one room covered with carpet and furnished with Western-style furniture.

Traditional-style restaurant in Tokyo

Only wealthy families in Japan have homes with central heating. (In many parts of the country, it really isn't needed.) Most rural families use electric or gas heaters for heat or cooking, in addition to their traditional hibachi. (A hibachi is an earthenware or metal pot in which charcoal is burned.)

Many Western-style appliances can be found in Japanese homes. Don't forget that Atari was a Japanese invention! And, of course, there are some very Japanese things, such as the *tokonoma* (nook) with its hanging scroll and flower arrangement.

SEAWEED, ANYONE?

The basic diet in Japan is changing as quickly as everything else. Some people may still have heaping bowls of rice with *miso* soup for breakfast. Younger people will probably have bread and eggs. But both groups will most likely drink tea.

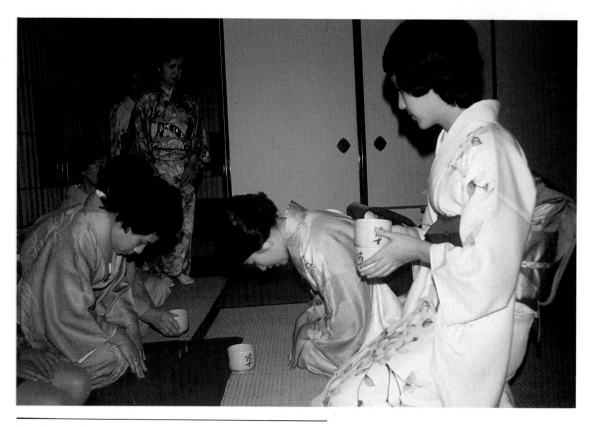

Bowing is a basic part of the tea ceremony called Chanoyu.

Miso soup, a favorite food, is made of seaweed (called kelp) stock or other soup stock in which soybean paste is dissolved. Diced soybean curd, vegetables, or other ingredients are added as supplementary solid food.

Tea and rice are still two important basics for Japanese meals. So is fish. Often Japanese people eat a certain kind of fish raw. After Westerners get up enough nerve to try raw fish, they usually admit that it's quite tasty.

The Japanese are learning to add more meat to their diet. But with land for raising animals so scarce, meat tends to be an imported, and thus more expensive, dish.

Traditional meals in Japan are served according to formal rules. Each person receives a tray. On the tray are many small bowls and dishes in a wide variety of shapes and sizes, each with only one kind of food in it. The Japanese people like to admire the color, texture, and design of each food. Western visitors find this agreeable. But they sometimes run into trouble when it comes time to eat that food—with chopsticks.

Most formal of all is the tea ceremony (called *Chanoyu*). It goes way back in Japanese history. In fact, *Chanoyu* is considered a form of art. The ceremony often takes place in a special teahouse in the garden. Guests are served two kinds of tea, thick and thin, with small sweet cakes. On occasion, an exquisite light meal is also served. The beauty of the garden, the teahouse, and the dishes are as important as the taste of the tea. The entire *Chanoyu* ceremony takes about four hours. It is another of those "islands of peace" that mean so much to the Japanese people.

SERIOUS ABOUT FUN

And how do Japanese people have fun? With the same energy and enthusiasm that they do everything else. Japanese people love sports. About a hundred years ago, an American teacher taught some pupils to play baseball. Now it's Japan's favorite sport and is played in high schools, colleges, two professional leagues, and even in the Japanese World Series.

Almost all kinds of sports, both traditional and modern, are popular in Japan. Traditional sports are *sumo* (Japanese wrestling), *judo*, *kendo* (Japanese fencing), and *kyudo* (Japanese archery).

But the Japanese also like to ski (on snow and water), skate, swim, bowl, hike, climb mountains, and play volleyball, football, soccer, golf, and table tennis.

Like people everywhere, the Japanese read, watch TV, and go to concerts, exhibits, and the theater. They enjoy vacations, both at home and in other countries. Often a large group of people—such

Sumo wrestlers face off (above). Sumo wrestling and baseball are Japan's most popular spectator sports. Opposite, children celebrate Buddha's birthday at a shopping center in Tokyo.

as a school class—will take a trip together. Japan's many beautiful parks offer them a lot to see and do.

But it is the festivals that are really special in Japan. The Japanese people seem to have a gift for celebrating things that other people too often take for granted. Three important holidays in Japan are New Year's Day (January 1), the emperor's birthday (April 29), and Constitution Day (May 3). There are a number of religious holidays. But the Japanese also observe many special occasions that aren't particularly religious or patriotic.

Fishermen celebrate the beginning of the fishing season. Everyone turns out to observe cherry blossom (or plum blossom or chrysanthemum) celebrations. A festival might be held just to look at the moon—and have fun—on a lovely summer night.

Girls have their own festival on March 3. They invite their friends over to see their beautiful dolls. Boys have their turn on

Carp streamers fly on Boys' Day, one for each son.

May 5. They display dolls of heroes and warriors. On a high pole
set in the garden or attached to the roof, paper or cloth streamers
in the shape of carp fly in the breeze—one for each son in the
house. Carp are considered a sign of strength and bravery.

A LAND ALIVE

Seaweed for breakfast and Kentucky Fried Chicken for lunch.
Jeans all day and a *yukata* in the evening. An Atari game followed
by a *sumo* wrestling match on TV. A noisy subway and a silent
garden. Life in Japan today is filled with contrasts. The powerful
forces from the past, such as love of nature, personal honor, and
respect for older people, are still important. But so are the
powerful forces of the future, such as technology and economic
competition with the rest of the world.

The past and the future meet in Japan. So do East and West. The
result is a colorful country, alive with both tradition and change.

Crowds stroll through the Ginza, the major shopping and entertainment area in downtown Tokyo.

MAP KEY

Place	Grid	Place	Grid	Place	Grid	Place	Grid
Abashiri	D12	Marugame	I6	Tochigi	H9	Kasukabe	n18
Aikawa	G9	Masuda	I5	Tokushima	I7	Katata	n14
Aizu-wakamatsu	H9	Matsue	I6	Tokuyama	I5	Katsuyama	m15
Aki	J6	Matsumae	F10	Tokyo	I9	Kawagoe	n18
Akita	G10	Matsumoto	H8	Tomakomai	E10	Kawaguchi	n18
Akkeshi	E12	Matsuyama	J6	Tottori	I7	Kawasaki	n18
Aomori	F10	Matsuzaka	I8	Tosa-shimizu	J6	Kinomoto	n15
Asahikawa	E11	Minamata	J5	Toyama	H8	Kiryu	m18
Atsuma	E10	Mishima	I9	Toyohashi	I8	Kisarazu	n19
Awa	J5	Mitake	I8	Tsu	I8	Kishiwada	o14
Beppu	J5	Mito	H10	Tsuchiura	H10	Kobe	o14
Bibai	E10	Miyako	G10	Tsuruga	I8	Kofu	n17
Chiba	I10	Miyakonojo	K5	Tsuruoka	G9	Koga	m18
Choshi	I10	Miyazaki	K5	Tsuyama	I6, 7	Kumagaya	m18
Ebetsu	E10	Mombetsu	D11	Ube	J5	Kumihama	n13
Embetsu	D10	Mori	E10	Ueda	H9	Kuwana	n15
Engaru	D11	Morioka	G10	Uji-yamada (Ise)	I8	Kyoto	o, n14
Fukagawa	E10, 11	Mount Fuji	I9	Uozu	H8	Maebashi	m18
Fukui	H8	Murakami	G9	Urawa	I9	Maizuru	n14
Fukuoka	F10	Muroran	E10	Ushibuka	J5	Mamba	m17
Fukuoka	J5	Muroto	J7	Utsunomiya	H9	Matsuida	m17
Fukushima	H10	Mutsu	F10	Uwajima	J6	Matsumoto	m16
Furano	E11	Nagano	H9	Wajima	H8	Matsuzaka	o15
Furukawa	H8	Nagaoka	H9	Wakayama	I7	Matsuzaki	o17
Gifu	I8	Nagasaki	J4	Wakkanai	D10	Mihama	o15
Gobo	J7	Nagoya	I8	Yaku (island)	K5	Mino	n15
Goshogawara	F10	Nakamura	J6	Yamagata	G10	Minokamo	n15
Goto Islands	J4	Nakatsu	J5	Yamaguchi	I5	Misakubo	n16
Haboru	D10	Nanao	H8	Yatsushiro	J5	Mishima	n18
Hachinohe	F10	Nayoro	D11	Yawatahama	J6	Mitake	n16
Hachioji	I9	Nemuro	E12	Yoichi	E10	Mito	m19
Hagi	I5	Nichinan	K5	Yokahama	I9	Mobara	n19
Hakodate	F10	Niigata	H9	Yokkaichi	I8	Motomachi	o18
Hamamatsu	I8	Niihama	J6	Yokoate (island)	L4	Mount Fuji (Fuji-san)	n17
Hama-tombetsu	D11	Niimi	I6	Yokosuka	I9	Mura	n18
Hanamaki	G10	Nikko	H9	Yokote	G10	Nagoya	n15
Higashiosaka	I7	Nobeoka	J5	Yonago	I6	Nakaminato	m19
Himeji	I7	Noboribetsu	E10	Yonezawa	H10	Nara	o14
Himi	H8	Nogata	J5	Yubari	E10	Narita	n19
Hiroo	E11	Noheji	F10			Neba	n16
Hirosaki	F10	Noshiro	F10			Nii (island)	o18
Hiroshima	I6	Numazu	I9	**MAP-INSET**		Nirasaki	n17
Hitachi	H10	Obihiro	E11			Nishio	o16
Hitoyoshi	J5	Odate	F10	Akechi	n16	Numazu	n17
Hofu	I5	Ofunato	G10	Amagasaki	o14	Oamishirasato	n19
Hombetsu	E11	Ogaki	I8	Amatsu-kominato	n19	Obama	n14
Ichinoseki	G10	Oita	J5	Anjo	o16	Odawara	n18
Iida	I8	Okaya	H9	Arai	o16	Ogaki	n15
Iizuka	J5	Okayama	I6	Ashikaga	m18	Okaya	m17
Iki (island)	J4	Oki Islands	H6	Asuke	n16	Omigawa	n19
Imabari	I6	Okushiri	E9	Atami	n18	Omiya	n18
Imabetsu	F10	Omiya	I9	Atsugi	n18	Omiya	o15
Ino	J6	Omuta	J5	Ayabe	n14	Osaka	o14
Isahaya	J5	Onomichi	I6	Chiba	n19	Otaki	n19
Ise (Uji-yamada)	I8	Osaka	I7	Chichibu	n18	Otsu	o14
Isesaki	H9	Oshamambe	E10	Chikura	o18	Otsuki	n17
Ishinomaki	G10	O-shima	J7	Choshi	n19	Oyama	m18
Itoigawa	H8	Otaru	E10	Daio	o15	Sabae	n15
Iwaki (Taira)	H10	Ozu	J6	Ena	n16	Sagara	o17
Iwakuni	I6	Rumoi	E10	Fuji	o17	Sakashita	n16
Iwamizawa	E10	Ryotsu	G9	Fujieda	o17	Sano	m18
Iwanai	E10	Sado (island)	G9	Fujinomiya	n17	Seto	n16
Izuhara	I4	Saga	J5	Fukuchiyama	n14	Shimada	o17
Izumo	I6	Saigo	H6	Fukushima	n16	Shimoda	o17
Kagoshima	K5	Saiki	J5	Funabashi	n19	Shimodate	m18
Kainan	I7	Sakata	G9	Furukawa	m16	Shimotsuma	m18
Kamaishi	G10	Samani	E11	Gamagori	o16	Shinshiro	o16
Kanazawa	H8	Sanjo	H9	Gero	n16	Shiojiri	m16
Kanoya	K5	Sapporo	E10	Gifu	n15	Shirotori	n15
Kanuma	H9	Sarufutsu	D11	Gojo	o14	Shitara	n16
Karatsu	J4	Sasebo	J4	Gotemba	n18	Shizuoka	o17
Kashiwazaki	H9	Sendai	G10	Hachioji	n18	Shuzenji	o17
Kasumi	I7	Sendai	K5	Hamamatsu	o16	Suzuka	o15
Kawasaki	I9	Setana	E9	Handa	o15	Tachikawa	n18
Kesennuma	G10	Seto	I8	Higashiizu	o18	Tajima	n16
Kii Strait	J7	Shibata	H9	Higashiosaka	o14	Takasaki	m17
Kinosaki	I7	Shibecha	E12	Hikone	n15	Takato	n17
Kiryu	H9	Shibetsu	D11	Hiratsuka	n18	Takatsuk	o14
Kita-ibaraki	H10	Shibetsu	E12	Hommura	o18	Takayama	m16
Kitakyushu	J5	Shikoku	J6	Ichikawa	n18	Takefu	n15
Kitami	E11	Shimabara	J5	Ichinomiya	n15	Tateyama	o18
Kobayashi	J, K5	Shimizu	I9	Iida	n16	Tenryu	o16
Kobe	I7	Shimonoseki	I5	Iijima	n16	To	o18
Kochi	J6	Shingu	J7	Ikeda	o14	Toba	o15
Kofu	I9	Shinjo	G10	Imazu	n15	Tochigi	m18
Komatsu	H8	Shiogama	G10	Ina	n16	Tokyo	n18
Komatsushima	I7	Shiroishi	G, H10	Ise	o15	Tomobe	m19
Koriyama	H10	Shizuoko	I9	Isesaki	m18	Toride	n19
Kozu (island)	I9	Sukumo	J6	Ishicka	m19	Toyohashi	o16
Kubokawa	J6	Sumoto	I7	Itami	o14	Toyonaka	o14
Kuji	F10	Suttsu	E10	Ito	o18	Toyota	n16
Kumamoto	J5	Taira (Iwaki)	H10	Kaizuka	o14	Tsu	o15
Kumano Bay	J8	Tajimi	I8	Kajikazawa	n17	Tsuchiura	m19
Kurashiki	I6	Takamatsu	I7	Kakegawa	o17	Tsuruga	n15
Kure	I6	Takaoka	H8	Kamakura	n18	Urawa	n18
Kurume	J5	Takara Islands	L, M4	Kameoka	o14	Ueda	m17
Kushimoto	J7	Takasaki	H9	Kamioka	m16	Ueno	o15
Kushiro	E12	Takayama	H8	Kanayama	n o	Wakayama	o14
Kuwana	I8	Takigawa	E10	Kariya	o15	Yaizu	o17
Kyoto	I7	Tamano	I6	Kashihara	o14	Yokkaichi	o15
Maebashi	H9	Tanabe	J7	Kashima	n19	Yokohama	n18
Maizuru	I7	Tateyama	I9			Yokoshiba	n19
Makurazaki	K5	Teshio	D10			Yokosuka	n18

MINI-FACTS AT A GLANCE

GENERAL INFORMATION

Official Name: Japan. The Japanese call their country Nippon or Nihon, which means "source of the sun."

Capital: Tokyo. In Japanese this means "eastern capital." Before 1868 Tokyo was called Edo, which means "estuary." Former capitals are Nara and Kyoto. (Kamakura was the capital of Yoritomo's military rule, or shogunate. During this time the emperor kept his capital in Kyoto.)

Language: Japanese. There are different ways of writing Japanese—*kanji, hiragana,* and *katakana.* School children also learn to write Japanese using the Roman alphabet. There are different ways of speaking Japanese, too. Intimate, polite, and honorific are three methods.

Government: Japan is a constitutional monarchy. There are three branches of government: executive, legislative, and judicial. The emperor is the symbol of the state, but does not rule the country. A prime minister is selected from the members of the Diet. The Diet consists of two houses. The House of Representatives has 511 members elected to four-year terms. The House of Councillors has 252 members elected to six-year terms. The country is divided into forty-seven prefectures. Each prefecture has a governor and assembly. The voting age is twenty years old. Women were given the right to vote in 1945.

Flag: The flag features a red circle (the sun) centered on a white background.

Imperial Family Crest: The crest features a golden chrysanthemum with sixteen petals.

National Song: *"Kimigayo"* ("The Reign of Our Emperor")

Religion: Japan has religious freedom. The Japanese native religion was Shinto, the worship of nature. It once became the state religion, but this was abolished after World War II. Other main religions are Buddhism and Christianity, Confucianism is not a religion, but it, along with Buddhism, has influenced the Japanese way of life greatly.

Money: Coins are of 1, 5, 10, 50, and 100 yen. Paper money is issued in bills of 100, 500, 1,000, 5,000, and 10,000 yen. One dollar in United States currency was worth about 125 yen in May, 1988. (The exchange rate varies every day under the floating system.)

Weights and Measures: Japan uses the metric system.

Population: 118 million (1981 census); 130,000,000 (1990 estimate)

Cities: About three fourths of the people live in cities. (Population based on 1987 figures.)

Tokyo 8,850,000
Yokohama 3,000,000
Osaka 2,795,000
Nagoya. 2,240,350
Kyoto 1,560,000
Sapporo 1,635,500
Kobe 1,495,493
Fukuoka 1,230,052
Kitakyushu 1,119,784
Kawasaki 1,100,000

Prefectures and Their Capitals:

		Miyagi	Sendai
Aichi	Nagoya	Miyazaki	Miyazaki
Akita	Akita	Nagano	Nagano
Aomori	Aomori	Nagasaki	Nagasaki
Chiba	Chiba	Nara	Nara
Ehime	Matsuyama	Niigata	Niigata
Fukui	Fukui	Oita	Oita
Fukuoka	Fukuoka	Okayama	Okayama
Fukushima	Fukushima	Okinawa	Naha
Gifu	Gifu	Osaka	Osaka
Gumma	Maebashi	Saga	Saga
Hiroshima	Hiroshima	Saitama	Urawa
Hokkaido	Sapporo	Shiga	Otsu
Hyogo	Kobe	Shimane	Matsue
Ibaraki	Mito	Shizuoka	Shizuoka
Ishikawa	Kanazawa	Tochigi	Utsunomiya
Iwate	Morioka	Tokushima	Tokushima
Kagawa	Takamatsu	Tokyo	Tokyo
Kagoshima	Kagoshima	Tottori	Tottori
Kanagawa	Yokohama	Toyama	Toyama
Kochi	Kochi	Wakayama	Wakayama
Kumamoto	Kumamoto	Yamagata	Yamagata
Kyoto	Kyoto	Yamaguchi	Yamaguchi
Mie	Tsu	Yamanashi	Kofu

GEOGRAPHY

Highest Point: Mount Fuji, an inactive volcano, 12,388 ft. (3,776 m)

Lowest Point: Sea level

Rivers: The Shinano, the longest river, is only 229 mi. (368 km) long. Japan has many short rivers that help produce electric power.

Lakes: Japan's largest lake is Lake Biwa, 265 sq. mi. (673.8 km²). There are many lakes in the craters of inactive volcanoes.

Seas and Oceans: The Sea of Japan lies to the west. East and south is the Pacific Ocean. North are the Sea of Okhotsk and the Pacific Ocean. Japan has its own sea called the Inland Sea.

Mountains: The highest mountain is Mount Fuji. Mountains and hills cover six sevenths of the land. The Japanese Alps have many high mountains. About 200 of Japan's mountains are volcanoes. Mount Aso is the world's largest active volcano.

Islands: Japan is made up of four main islands: Honshu, Hokkaido, Kyushu, and Shikoku. About 3,000 small islands lie in the Inland Sea. Japan owns a chain of about 100 islands called the Ryukyus. Okinawa is the largest of the Ryukyus. The 97 Bonin Islands are also owned by Japan.

Bays: Japan has hundreds of bays. The largest, Tokyo Bay, is 30 mi. (48 km) long. Other large bays include Ise Bay, Osaka Bay, Tosa Bay, Toyama Bay, and Uchiura Bay.

Earthquakes: There are nearly 1,500 small earthquakes each year. In 1923 an earthquake killed 99,331 persons and 43,476 were reported missing. The earthquake that struck Niigata in 1964 killed 30 persons and caused a great deal of damage.

Climate: The climate varies throughout Japan. Kyushu and Shikoku have hot summers and mild winters. Honshu has warm, wet summers and mild winters in the south, but cold, snowy winters in the north. Hokkaido has cool summers and cold, snowy winters. It seldom snows in Tokyo. In early summer and early fall heavy rains called monsoons hit Japan. Other storms called typhoons also strike.

Coastline: The four main islands have coastlines totaling 5,857 mi. (9,426 km).

Area: 145,834 sq. mi. (377,708 km²)

NATURE:

Trees: Forests cover about two thirds of Japan. Trees include cedar, maple, oak, pine, mulberry, poplar, and willow. Fruit trees include apple, peach, orange, tangerine, plum, and cherry.

Flowers: The favorite flower is the cherry blossom. Other flowers include: chrysanthemums, irises, tulips, forsythia, violets, morning glories, peonies, camellias, roses, daffodils, poppies, hollyhocks, rose of Sharon, bush-clover, lotus, Easter lilies and water lilies, and orchids.

Birds: Japan has many birds, including geese, ducks, hawks, eagles, quail, pheasant, plover gulls, cormorants, swans, storks, herons, cranes, crows, starlings, owls, whippoorwills, swallows, nightingales, cuckoos, woodpeckers, larks, bobolinks, wrens, and sparrows.

Insects: Butterflies, moths, dragonflies, houseflies, bees, crickets, grasshoppers, cicadas, mosquitoes, gnats, and fireflies

Animals: Wild animals include deer, bears, and monkeys. Farm animals are usually small because farms are small. Common farm animals are pigs and chickens. Only a few farms have room for cows. Pets include cats, dogs, parrots, goldfish, hamsters, and chipmunks.

EVERYDAY LIFE:

Food: Fish is the main source of protein. Most fish is eaten cooked, but a few particular kinds of fresh fish can be eaten raw as a delicacy called "sashimi." Rice is the basic food. Meals are eaten off trays with each food placed in a separate bowl. Japanese use chopsticks. Breakfast can be a bowl of rice with *miso* soup or bread and eggs. *Miso* soup is made of broth, soybean paste, and vegetables or seaweed. Tea is the favorite drink. The *Chanoyu* (tea ceremony) is a ceremonial tea drinking in a special teahouse.

Homes: In the countryside, houses are small, one- or two-story structures made of wood or cement with thatched or tiled roofs. In cities people own houses and apartments. Traditional houses have sliding paper doors. Straw mats (tatami) cover the floors. Tables are low. Quilts are spread on the floor. Only wealthy families have central heating. Most families use electric or gas heaters or the traditional hibachi. A special nook (*tokonoma*) holds a hanging scroll and flower arrangement.

Clothing: Although many Japanese wear Western-style clothes, some still wear traditional clothes. The kimono is a long, loose robe with a sash called an *obi*. Wooden sandals called *geta* or rubber-soled sandals called *zori* are removed at the entrance of a house and slippers are worn to walk on corridors, but not inside the rooms.

Customs: The Japanese respect age, bravery, and loyalty. They are very polite to each other.

Holidays:
> January 1, New Year's Day
> January 15, Adulthood Day
> February 11, Commemoration of the Founding of the Nation
> March 3, Girls' Day
> March 21 or 22, Vernal Equinox Day
> April 29, Emperor's Birthday
> May 3, Constitution Day
> May 5, Boys' Day (Children's Day)
> September 15, Respect for the Aged Day
> September 23 or 24, Autumnal Equinox Day
> October 10, Health-Sports Day
> November 3, Culture Day
> November 23, Labor-Thanksgiving Day

Art: Buddhism had an influence upon Japanese painting. Paintings called "Sumie," black-ink brush painting on white background, were done on scrolls for several hundred years. Later, wood-block prints also became popular.

Sculpture: Sculpture was done in wood, but also bronze or clay. Many sculptures were created of Buddha.

Music: Traditional music is played on *fue* (woodwind instrument), *shakuhachi* (a type of flute, *koto* (stringed instrument), *biwa* (like a mandolin), *shamisen* (like a banjo), gongs, cymbals, and hand drums. Traditional music may sound strange to Westerners. Tokyo has seven symphony orchestras. Popular music from the West is popular with the Japanese.

Theater: Two traditional Japanese dramatic forms are *No*, developed in the 1300s for noble audiences, and *kabuki*, developed for popular audiences. Men perform women's roles in *kabuki* drama.

Poetry: Famous types of Japanese poetry are waka and haiku. *Waka* poems contain 31 syllables and *haiku*, 17 syllables. Waka express various human emotions and haiku mainly describe nature.

Crafts: Traditional Japanese crafts include lacquer boxes, silk weaving, pottery making, cloisonné (enameling), carvings, and flower arranging. Origami (paper folding) is also a traditional art taught to young children at school.

Recreation: Japanese enjoy traditional and Western plays, movies, and television programs. About 98.5 percent of families have color TV sets. Almost all families have radios. Japanese often take trips to the countryside or to other countries in large groups.

Sports: The most popular sport is baseball. Also popular are soccer, football, swimming, skiing, skating, bowling, hiking, mountain climbing, volleyball, golf, and table tennis. Traditional Japanese sports include *sumo* wrestling, judo (self-defense martial art), *kendo* (fencing), and *kyudo* (archery).

Communications: The government owns the telephone, telegraph, and postal systems. Japan has about 180 daily newspapers. Circulation is the second highest in the world.

Transportation: Trains are the most popular form of transportation. The world's fastest trains travel between Tokyo and Osaka at speeds up to 130 mi. (210 km) per hour. About two of every five families own a car. There are 685,959 mi. (1,103,709 km) of road. About 293,353 mi. (472,005 km) are paved. All major cities have an airport. Kobe is the busiest seaport in Japan. Japan has the second largest merchant fleet in the world.

Education: Japan has compulsory education. All children must attend six years of elementary school and three years of junior high school. If students pass an entrance examination, they may attend three years of senior high school. Japan has over 1,000 colleges and universities, of which 128 were established by the government. Some elementary schoolchildren and most high school students wear uniforms—blue middy tops and skirts for girls and blue or black jackets with stand-up collars and the same color trousers for boys. More than 99 percent of the people can read and write.

What People Do for a Living: More than 34 percent of the workers are involved in manufacturing; about 18 percent, wholesale and retail trade; 3 percent, banking and insurance; 9 percent, construction; 6 percent, transportation and communication; 9 percent, agriculture and forestry; 4 percent, government; 1 percent, fishing; 1 percent, mining and utilities; 15 percent, services. Japanese workers receive many benefits, including cash bonuses, inexpensive housing, company stores, medical care, recreational facilities, and guaranteed work for life. About 40 percent of Japan's employed workers are women.

Principal Products:
Agriculture: Barley, fruits, potatoes, rice, soybeans, tea, tobacco, wheat
Fishing: Flounder, mackerel, pike, salmon, sardines, shellfish, tuna, whales
Manufacturing: Ceramics, chemicals, electronic products, iron, steel, lenses, cameras, machinery, motor vehicles, ships, textiles
Mining: Coal, copper, iron, lead, manganese, sulfur, zinc

Principal Imports: Coal, crude oil, food, iron ore, machinery, wood, raw cotton, wool, and copper

Principal Exports: Chemicals, electronic equipment, iron, steel, motor vehicles, ships, textiles, TV sets, radios, tape recorders, and watches

Farmland: Only about 15 percent of the land can be used for farming, yet Japan produces almost three fourths of her needed food. The average farm is only about 2.4 acres (1 hectare).

IMPORTANT DATES

660 B.C. — Jimmu Tenno becomes emperor

A.D. 57 — First recorded contact with China

350 — The Yamato clan becomes the most powerful clan

552 — Buddhism introduced to the Japanese

593-628 — Empress Suiko reigns

604 — Seventeen Article Constitution written

646 — The Great Reform Period begins

673-686 — Emperor Temmu reigns

712 — The *Kojiki* written

720 — The *Nihongi* written

781-806 — Emperor Kammu reigns

794 — Emperor sets up capital in Kyoto

1160 — Taira family takes political control from the Fujiwaras

1185 — The Minamotos defeat the Tairas

1192 — Yoritomo appointed shogun

1274 — Kublai Khan attempts to invade Japan

1281 — Kublai Khan's fleet wiped out by *Kamikaze*

1338-1573 — Ashikaga family of shoguns rules

1543 — Portuguese arrive in Japan

1549—St. Francis Xavier introduces Christianity to Japan

1592—Japan invades Korea

1597—Christians executed by Hideyoshi

1600—Dutch ships arrive in Japan

1603—Edo becomes the site of the Tokugawa Shogunate; Tokugawas become actual rulers

1614—Christian priests forced to leave Japan

1637—Christian rebellion occurs in Kyushu and thousands of Christians are killed; the Japanese are forbidden to leave Japan

1639—All European traders except the Dutch ordered out of Japan

1707—Mount Fuji erupts for the last time

1853—Commodore Mathew C. Perry reaches Japan

1858—Japan and the United States sign treaties

1867—The Tokugawas defeated by the Emperor's supporters; Emperor Meiji becomes ruler

1868—Tokyo becomes capital of Japan; Keio University founded

1870—Shinto proclaimed the official religion; *Mainichi,* the first Japanese newspaper, published

1872—First railroad built from Tokyo to Yokohama

1873—Ban on Christianity ended

1875—Doshisha University founded in Kyoto

1877—Tokyo Imperial University founded

1878—Bonin Islands become property of Japan

1880—New criminal code written

1882—Waseda University founded

1889—The constitution written

1890—New civil code written

1894-1895—China and Japan at war

1904—Japan declares war on Russia

1905—Russia and Japan sign Treaty of Portsmouth

1906—South Manchurian Railway begun

1910—Korea becomes a Japanese colony

1914-1918 — Japan fights World War I

1919 — Japan becomes one of the Big Five world powers

1920 — Japan becomes a member of League of Nations; Japan signs the Nine-Power Treaty and the London Naval Treaty

1923 — Earthquakes strikes Tokyo and Yokohoma

1931 — The Manchurian incident breaks out

1932 — Japanese conquer Manchuria and change its name to Manchukuo

1933 — Japan walks out of League of Nations

1937 — Japan and China at war (The China Incident begins)

1941 — Japan attacks Pearl Harbor on December 7, starting World War II; the United States and Japan declare war

1942 — Japan loses battles at Midway and Guadalcanal

1944 — Showa Shinzan, a volcano, first erupts

1945 — Hiroshima atomic-bombed on August 6; Nagasaki atomic-bombed on August 9; emperor surrenders on September 2

1947 — New constitution goes into effect

1951 — Japan signs peace treaty with forty-eight other countries

1952 — Japan tries to join the United Nations; occupation of Japan ends

1956 — Russia and Japan sign treaty to end war and start diplomatic relations; Japan allowed to join the United Nations

1960 — Japan and the United States sign Treaty of Mutual Cooperation and Security

1964 — Earthquake wrecks Niigata; Summer Olympics held in Tokyo

1970 — Japan launches a space satellite

1971 — U.S. President Richard Nixon and Emperor Hirohito meet in Anchorage, Alaska

1972 — Okinawa returned to Japan

1981 — Japan agrees to limit automobile exports to West Germany, Canada, and the United States

1983 — Japan remains one of the most important manufacturing nations in the world

1986 — A Japanese spacecraft skirts Halley's Comet; the Suisei sends back pictures and scientific data

1987 — Susumu Tonegawa becomes the first Japanese citizen to win the Nobel Prize for medicine in honor of his studies of the body's immune system

1988—The Seikan train tunnel opens; the 33.46 mile tunnel is the longest in the world

1989—Crown Prince Akihito becomes the 125th emperor of the Chrysanthemum Throne upon the death of his father, Emperor Hirohito

1991—Kiichi Miyazawa becomes prime minister, succeeding Toshike Kaifu; Mount Unzen, a volcano dormant for at least two centuries, erupts, killing at least 38

IMPORTANT PEOPLE

Kobo Abe (1924-   ), writer, born in Tokyo

Emperor Akihito (1933-   ), born in Tokyo

Ryunosuke Akutagawa (1892-1927), author of *Rashomon*, born in Tokyo

Matsuo Basho (1648-1694), pseudonym for Munefusa Matsou, haiku poet, born in Ueno

Yosa Buson (1716-1781), haiku poet, born in Settsu

Monzaemon Chikamatsu (1653-1724), Kabuki playwright, born in Echizen

Leo Esaki (1925-   ), shared the 1973 Nobel Prize in physics, born in Osaka

Emperor Hirohito (1901-1989), born in Tokyo

Katsushika Hokusai (1760-1849), painter, born in Tokyo

Hirobumi Ito (1841-1909), born in Choshu

Jimmu Tenno (reigned 660-585 B.C.), the first legendary emperor of Japan, born in Kyushu

Kakinomoto-no-Hitomaro (655-709), poet, birthplace unknown

Yasunari Kawabata (1899-1972), writer, winner of the 1968 Nobel Prize in literature, born in Osaka

Shibasaburo Kitasato (1852-1931), scientist, born in Kumamoto

Issa Kobayashi (1763-1827), haiku poet, born in Kashiwabara

Akira Kurosawa (1910-   ), film director, born in Tokyo

Toshiro Mifune (1920-   ), star of Japanese films, born in Chingtao, China

Yukio Mishima, pseudonym for Hiraoka Kimitake, (1925-1970), novelist, born in Tokyo

Kenji Mizoguchi (1898-1956), film director, born in Tokyo

Murasaki Shikibu (974-1031), wrote *Genji Monogatari*, birthplace unknown

Emperor Mutsuhito (known as Emperor Meiji) (1852-1912), born in Kyoto

Empress Nagako (1903-   ), born in Tokyo

Hideyo Noguchi (1876-1928), scientist, born in Inawashiro

Seiji Ozawa (1935-   ), symphony orchestra conductor, born in Hoten

Yasujiro Ozu (1903-1963), film director, born in Tokyo

Eisaku Sato (1901-1975), prime minister, winner of 1974 Nobel Peace Prize, born in Yamaguchi

Sei Shonagon (966-1013), wrote *Makura no soshi,* born in Kyoto

Kenzo Tange (1913-   ), architect, born in Osaka

Junichiro Tanizaki (1886-1965), novelist, born in Tokyo

Hideki Tojo (1884-1948), prime minister, born in Tokyo

Sin-itiro Tomonaga (1906-1979), shared the 1965 Nobel Prize in physics, born in Kyoto

Hideyoshi Toyotomi (1536-1598), military leader, born in Aichi

Isoroku Yamamoo (1884-1943), navy admiral, born in Niigata

Tomoyuki Yamashita (1885-1946), army general, born in Kochi

Hideki Yukawa (1907-1981), scientist, winner of the Nobel Prize in physics, born in Tokyo

Children picking the fruit of a persimmon tree

INDEX

Page numbers that appear in boldface type indicate illustrations

125

About the Author

Carol Greene has a B.A. in English Literature from Park College, Parkville, Missouri and an M.A. in Musicology from Indiana University, Bloomington. She's worked with international exchange programs, taught music and writing, and edited children's books. She now works as a freelance writer in St. Louis, Missouri and has had published over 20 books for children and a few for adults. When she isn't writing, Ms. Greene likes to read, travel, sing, and do volunteer work at her church. Her other books for Childrens Press include: *The Super Snoops and the Missing Sleepers; Sandra Day O'Connor: First Woman on the Supreme Court; Rain! Rain!; Please, Wind?; Snow Joe;* and *The New True Book of Holidays Around the World.*